From the Enchanted Waters to the Waters of Illusion:

The Rio São Francisco Transposition Case

Loreley Garcia (Coordinator)
Oswaldo Giovannini Jr.
Mayrinne Meira Wanderley

Rockville
2017

1st Edition

GlobalSouth
P R E S S

For more information, please contact
info@globalsouthpress.com or go to
http://www.globalsouthpress.com/

From the Enchanted Waters to the Waters of Illusion

Copyright © 2016 by
GARCIA, Loreley; GIOVANNINI JR.,
Oswaldo; MEIRA WANDERLEY, Mayrinne
1st ed. — Rockville — 2017

Includes bibliographical references and index

ISBN: 978-1-943350-57-5
Library of Congress Control Number: 2017931843
1. Social Sciences — Anthropology / Cultural & Social
2. Social Sciences— Developing & Emerging Countries
3. International Studies — Brazil

In other words, I would like to be a crocodile living in the São Francisco River. I would like to be a crocodile, because I love the great rivers, because they are deep as the man's soul. On the surface they are very lively and clear, but at the deep bottom they are quiet and dark as the sufferings of men. Another thing I also love about our great rivers: their eternity. Yes, river is a magic word to describe *eternity.*

(João Guimarães Rosa, "The time and the turn of Augustus Matraga" Sagarana).

Summary

Chapter III: The Struggles 85

Conclusion: Another look at life on Earth: a civilization without transpositions 109

Referências 135

Acknowledgments

This project was only possible thanks to funds received by CAPES through the National Postdoctoral Program, to develop Project *No Reservations* 2011/2016, 2584/2011 public notice, in the sociology department.

We thank the Truká people, from Assunção Island, especially Claudia Truká, Bino, Josivaldo, Maurílio who received, guided us through the villages and helped conduct the interviews and workshops. To Pipipã people, to Chief Valdemir who also guided us and made it possible to visit the villages.

To the PNPD ex-alumni who participated in the execution of this research, Cassandra Veras, Tulio Rossi and Rodrigo Cruz Gagliano, who reviewed the text.

To the researchers and explorers who interviewed, under the caatinga sun, the young and key people of Truká villages, and participated in the workshops that our team offered for Truká villages: Valeria Dantas Araújo, Edilon Mendes Nunes, Lorena L.C. Monteiro, Livia Freire.

To Professor Parry Scott, of the Federal University of Pernambuco, who provided us with several important contacts to be received by Truká tribe.

To the Integration Ministry and to the engineer Jorge Kiyoshi for the granted interviews.

To José Guilherme Amaral, actor and director of Paraiban theater, who provided a theater workshop to young people of OJIT.

To the members of the Caravana *contra a transposição* who brought their relentless struggle for our city and university.

To the magnificent São Francisco River, the Opará that inspired this work and all the struggles of survival that, despite all attempts, keeps its magic eternity!

ILLUSTRATIONS Alberto Ricardo Pessoa

COVER Roberto Mario Castelo

PREFACE

The transmutation of the Enchanted Waters in Waters of Illusions

Everybody sings the wonders of the great river and take their hat off, revering the Old Chico. The river there, in the outback, is only known as São Francisco. Soap Operas about the Old Chico enact romance novels in its sands and farms, invade the homes of Brazil, all moved by audience research, without hurting the sponsors, while rivers dry up, the fishes disappear and sand replaces the water. But the dams are there, like huge shallow mirrors, it's the waters that elude visitors. The dams give an idea of being plenty, the water as a memory in the belly of peasants with schistosomiasis, with its thin members pouring in a cachectic body hanging from an exuberant belly that foretells its death. The São Francisco looks like a very much loved river, that does not know it can imagine itself well saved by this love sung in verse and prose. But "quá"! Not quite like that. Manuelzão Nardi, cowboy who ran the Silga farm[1] in Andrequicé district of Três Marias, near Rio de Janeiro, used to say he was very afraid of untrue love. So, close to a full eighty years of age, when a journalist asked him if he was afraid to die, while he was going for a stomach surgery, he said: "I'm not afraid of death because I know I will die one day; what I fear is untrue love that kills apart from God's will."

The hinterland man is good but suspicious. The lands and the waters of São Francisco attracted adventurers and traders wanting to make money or to hide from the police. I remember like it was yesterday, a rustic hinterland woman, intelligent, illiterate, widow and plenty of children, who became a friend through the passing of time. One day, when I saw her receiving a compliment from a neighbor,

---

1   The farm was from a cousin of Guimarães Rosa, Manuelzão met there the writer and with him he traveled ten days leading cattle, and was later the character in the book *A festa do Manuelzão*.

I commented: this 'compadre' there seems to really like you. And she was instantaneous: - he likes me like a shotgun likes a Tupinambis! He wants to buy my land at a cheap price.

Old Chico has known stories, lost stories, sometimes, unburied stories, as in karst caves of Lagoa Santa in Minas Gerais, on the margins of the Rio das Velhas, where bones of human and animals of giant fauna rest. The nomadic people already knew the São Francisco valley for thousands of years, as the people called Cariri. They transited from Ceará to the valley, assembling traps for animals to be delighted in the meals, making hunting stories, funeral ceremonies and love scenes in those starry clean skies with wonderful moonlights, where they camped, hunted and collected. In 1500, the coastal ones spotted some caravels and everything changed. At first, they rejoiced, even being a little frightened, hardly knowing that a disaster would befall them, with those strange and powerful travelers. Another culture had just arrived. Imagine the impact on the land being invaded by other civilizations? They would acquaint the Jesuits, Franciscans, Capuchins, traders and Portuguese rulers. They had to run from dogs and walk while chained. Separated from their children that were taken to catechesis school, where they mocked the old gods and ancestral beliefs.

Centuries are hard to pass, but when they do, it seems that was in a blink of an eye. Progress comes with monocultures of sugar cane and sugar mills. Grass on the farms of the drovers, endless eucalyptus trees, all kinds of fruit, corn, beans, castor beans, soybeans, expanding exports. But the water was gone. Where's the water, the charm of life? When executives jets, businesses and banks pass on Três Marias and Sobradinho, entrepreneurs say to the governments: - look how many water and how many land. We can build more irrigation canals and deeper wells, we have fertile land, dams and plenty of water. Look at that huge lagoon, imagine there a plantation of watermelons? And their manly breasts fills with pride of this great country that has no more surubins, forests and jaguars as before. But up there everything is apparent, there is no one to contradict, it is easy to sell projects in Brasilia. And they know they will not pay for the use of water, because the basin committee controlled by ANA and AGB Dead Fish agency guarantees this courtesy.

The death surrounds the São Franciscan ecosystems. Its aquifers waning, disappearing with the base flow that supported life in the waters of rivers, which are now beginning to be temporary, while multiplying dams and wells accumulating water in larger properties. In a well-known restaurant in the historic Penedo, where Maurice of Nassau used to live and cruise ships arrived, I ate, a few years ago, Amazonian surubim acquired in Maceio and Aracaju markets. In all, to the waiter one can ask for Tilapia (Egyptian) treated with food there in the sight, in the "farms" or surrounded in the river or fish from the sea. The river there is another bionic channel that drains water from hydroelectrics, which tourists love to see when walking in catamaran on Xingó Lake, with its green waters!

Deforestation has drastically reduced biodiversity of the basin, dried up lagoons and paths, the surubins survivors cry in the back of the dark rivers in Bahia and Minas Gerais, remembering the sadness of human beings, in this contradictory unity of interest between prey and predators. There is fire everywhere, poisons with high contaminating power are launched in plantations by aircraft. Urban, domestic, industrial and farms sewers run through the rivers. Miners dig riverbeds and rivers to export the raw material.

Since the second half of the twentieth century until today, three new executioners arrived with force: first, the hydroelectrics, changing the dynamics of the rivers, especially that flooded the oxbow lakes, taking from the riverines traditional forms of agricultural survival as the ebb agriculture and access to fish, which guaranteed them independent living; then came the outbreak of irrigation projects from agribusiness export *of commodities,* which at one point joined the devastating cycle of exportation of iron ore to China. The São Francisco basin is lowered, it is in throes: and state and federal executives, the Supreme Court and the National Congress have still approved or made "deaf ears", to the absurd that was the transposition project of São Francisco. That is bait, a white elephant, a technical fraud, an unburied monument of incompetence and corruption, who lives will see and remember.

The historical review of Professor Loreley Garcia's team, listening to Truká people about the effects of the transposition, that repeats the clash of cultures over more than 500 years ago, is a plus

13

component of popular and academic resistance in this initiative of the drought industry, deviating the country's resources for unnecessary constructions. But the most perverse product of the drought industry took place in the regional mentality. To extort federal money, the colonels of the drought industry planted, in the Northeast and in the federal capitals in these centuries, the culture of government dependency, poverty as a destination, the permanent call for help, the misconception that nothing goes right there, whether by land quality or by the lack of water. They hid from the people the abundance, the potential, the extreme value of the caatinga and the cerrado, the colossal adaptation of its flora and fauna, the positive aspects of the sun on its beaches as tourism attractiveness, besides the rich handicrafts, musicality and happiness of local people, the sweet taste of their native fruits.

The Northeast is a splendor, bad, ugly, even cruel, it is the face of the the elite that until here exploit the drought industry, becoming the greater cause of poverty in the Northeast.

Apolo Heringer Lisboa
M.D, creator of Manuelzão Project. He conceived and coordinated the 2007 Caravan in defense of São Francisco, the semi-arid and against Transposition.

Presentation

Eternity called into question, or *"Supra, praeter vei contra naturam"*.

In August of 2007, I was in the OAB/PB Auditorium, to receive the Caravan in Defense of Rio São Francisco and Semi-Arid against the Transposition of São Francisco river. At that time I first heard Professor Apolo Heringer Lisboa associate the existence of the São Francisco River to the idea of a miracle:

> The São Francisco is a miracle of nature, it "runs on the contrary": instead of going to Southeast, West or South, like other rivers in the region, it heads to the Northeast, due to a geological fault called "Sãofranciscana Depression." Its historical importance is unique because it served as a way into the country and link between the Southeast and Northeast. For there it brought water, fertility, people, work, food, energy , beauty, culture, history ... was regarded as "river of national unity" [2] .

But what is a miracle? In the most common sense, miracle (from Latim the *miraculum* , *mirare* verb - "marvel" with a stupendous fact) is an extraordinary event that has no scientific explanation and that seems to violate the natural laws governing ordinary phenomena. Tomás de Aquino created a classic concept for the miracle: "It's something superior, different, or contrary to nature, *"Supra, praeter vei contra naturam. "*

So, how could a river, an integral part of nature, be against nature?

Instead of giving the miracle the Judeo-Christian meaning or Islamic, I propose to rescue the meaning of the 'Greek miracle', or the moment in which philosophers stopped explaining the world and its origin through the mythology and began to seek explanations for

---

2   Available in: http://saofranciscovivo.org.br/site/wp-content/uploads/2014/12/panfleto-pau-de-colher.pdf.

nature *(physis)* within the nature itself. Instead of the myth, the rational and philosophical thought began to reveal the primordial and original founding of the *physis* - what is born, sprout, grow and produce. *Physis* is usually translated as Nature, but the translation is inaccurate, because *physis* concerns the origin of everything that exists and to its essence, manifested in the movement[3]. The *physis* expresses the principle of movement, it refers to the act of making up the things that change appearance, but remain always being the same, changing to keep the form, order and stability.

Author of the Greek miracle, the first philosopher, Thales of Miletus, also believed that water was the *"dynamis"*, the creative power of the world. The miracle appears linked to water. Also in the Bible, the creationist myth, water is the only element that creates and is not created in seven days. At that time, Professor Lisboa, described the situation of the river-miracle:

> A doomed river. These 506 years of history have also been years of abuse, depredation and death. It is not a surprise that the Old Chico is each day closer to extinction.
>
> Because it is seen only as "water resources" and its basin as if it were an inexhaustible "building material deposit", which can take without resetting, without care. From the cattle corrals, through navigation, predatory fishing, hydroelectrics, irrigation, mining, until the current transposition project, the complex life that is São Francisco is being destroyed to be transformed into easy and capital profits. Deforestation, siltation, pollution (domestic, industrial, agricultural) condemn it. This year, it was almost interrupted in some places and its historical source dried up. The lack of rain just revealed more of his state of penury[4].

---

3   "Everything that is born is destined to be what it should be and nothing else. This birth for at which it rises is subjected to a process of realization, is the phýsis, and as such, the Arche. [...] Both the physis and the Arche are not expressions of anarchic [...] nor the occasional... What do these terms jointly designate is what happens always or ordinary [...] but with an effectiveness such that always "triggers" (like a biological trigger) which is best of all possible" (SPINELLI, Miguel. Questões Fundamentais da Filosofia Grega. São Paulo: Loyola, 2006, pp.36-37).

4   Panfleto Pau de Colher (2014), Articulação Popular São Francisco Vivo, accessed on September 10, 2014 at http://saofranciscovivo.org.br/site/wp-content/uploads/2014/12/panfleto-pau-de- colher.pdf .

In this book, the authors propose to discuss the current condition of the river and the implementation of a project that, for many, will mean their condemnation, or how a miracle-river becomes a dying river, when it loses its strengths and potentials and is brought to an irreversible point, and, probably, will lead the ecosystems and the people who depend on it to survive, to the same destination.

This book presents results based on the "*No Reservations*" research, held between 2012 and 2016, with funds from the National Program for Postdoctoral studies, PNPD/Capes. In it, we announced the results of the second part of the project, which involved the study of two traditional populations affected by the work of transposition. The research was performed in Cabrobó (2013-2015) and Ibimirim (2016), both counties in Pernambuco, in the first one, the water was removed, which would travel the north axis of transposition, and in the second is cut by channels of eastern transposition axis.

To compose the text, we were inspired in the sequence adopted by the book «Os Sertões». In Chapter 1, we describe the land and the river, the origins, reasons, and critical developments of the São Francisco river transposition project, now renamed with a more palatable name: Integration Project with the basins of the Septentrional Northeast.

In Chapter 2, the impact of the project is terminated by one of the people who inhabited the margins of the river for at least 300 years, being the most affected by this developmental construction. Here they express their visions and speak about their feelings concerned to their river and their world.

Chapter 3 talks about the dimensions of the fight against the implementation of the São Francisco River Integration Project (PISF) from the legal fight until the social movements that integrated the Caravan in Defense of Rio São Francisco and the struggle of indigenous peoples, especially the resistance of Truká.

We started the presentation highlighting the scenario and responsible characters for the implementation of the transposition project that, in our view, is configured as a legitimate checkmate to the river, accelerating its destruction.

Loreley Garcia
Coordinator of Project *No Reservations*
October, 2016

Introduction: Scenery and Circumstances

> In 2010, a poor Northeast person will make what not even an emperor could[5].

The political scientist Bolivar Lamounier[6] analysis a particularly interesting aspect of the Brazilian political scene: the permanence of Sebastianism and the savior myth. To him, it is a cultural predisposition in heritage from the Portuguese metropolis. The idea of the Savior refers to the emergence of a leader who had a mission to repair injustices and outrages, leveraging the society to a higher level of development and prosperity. The idea of a savior undermines the fundamental principles of democratic tradition, which is the collective participation that defines and leads the destinies of nations. Put in the hands of a savior the destinies of a plural collectivity to decide and perform actions that affect all, is the brand of populist and authoritarian regimes. Brazil is not a country with a democratic tradition, our history shows that the call Salvationists, in the past and in the present, and had no trouble adjusting to the political scene, both in speeches of the right and left.

Lamounier also points out that the Portuguese colonization left us one patrimonial state, "a state structure headed by bureaucracy and by politicians specialized in co-opt groups of interest to, together, 'suck the teats' of the state in name of the interests of small circles of economic power"[7].

Pursuing the analysis, he teaches that the patrimonialist state was modified and began to incorporate corporatism. Thus, what was previously restricted to politicians and businessmen, got extended to various sectors of society, such as the pro-management unions, which started to act as interest groups nurtured by the state manna that flows in the form of public resources. In a cynical view, we could say that there has been a democratization of patrimonialism.

---

5   Lula Speech in the 2006 campaign - Reviewed by Veja magazine (11/12/2015).
6   Magazine Special Exame, May of 2016.
7   Idem.

The combination of patrimonialism with corporatism was added to the figure of a charismatic leader, who embodied the figure of the savior in the style of redeeming Sebastianism, and the manicheism originated from a low Marxism that would serve to try to convince society that the world was divided between ‹we, the people› and ‹they, the elite›, always fighting until one side is defeated. This discourse, which combines messianism to the traditional doctrine of the left, was retaken after the fall of the military dictatorship, under the belief that the country would be ready and eager to adopt a left policy.

To Lamounier[8], the ends to be achieved are three: the protection of the poor, the relentless fight against elites and the defense of national sovereignty. We could think about a kind of distributive nationalism. The three principles, above any suspicions, have the power to confer ethical superiority front of opponents/other/cons/elites. But, the great danger, the author points out, is that the populist once legitimized by the vote, treats the whole country like a personal property and justifies all his actions in the name of saving the poor. This is already a breeding ground for the creation of charismatic populist leader or a poor imitation of a tyrant.

"Lula acted as if Brazil was his property"[9]

Developments and Involvement

> The historical background of Lula reminds the historical background of the São Francisco river itself: many sources cleaned at the head of the fountain, after a bumpy path, many spoils, silting and contradictory alliances along the way; the lure of the big capital in its final course; the withering away, as river and as political history, without reaching the ocean of emotional memory of the Brazilian people. The history of popular leadership of Lula is the story of a failure ... (Paulo Maldoz)[10].

---

8 Idem.
9 Folha de São Paulo, 05.29.2016, p. C-9.
10 President Lula and Dom Cappio in Roda Viva History In: Dias, Deborah; Castro, Gigi; Said, Magnolia; Gonçalves, Adelaide (Org). **A vida por um rio**.

"In 2003, the first Lula government, despite internal conflicts, chose to maintain a traditional left-wing discourse and to rescue an agenda based on national developmentalism in the years 1950/60. "

To Marcos Lisboa[11] in 2009, it was adopted a 'great Brazil' project, following the same model of the 'Second National Development Plan' in the government of Ernesto Geisel (1975). Perhaps, lacking innovative ideas, the left policy, after decades fighting the military dictatorship, copies its development project: construct great buildings, known as pharaonic, completely disregarding the environmental damage, ecological demands that reconfigure the political struggles in XXI century[12].

The Superintendence for the Development of the Northeast (SUDENE), created in 1959 by President Juscelino Kubitschek (1956-61), had as its founder and first economist superintendent Celso Furtado, with the aim of developing the Northeast based on investments in infrastructure constructions and tax incentives for companies that would install themselves there. Celso Furtado was impeached by the military dictatorship in 1964, and SUDENE became a business involved with corruption, clientelism service and fostering drought industry.

In 2001, after several irregularity scandals, the SUDENE was abolished by President Fernando Henrique Cardoso. In January 2007, the Lula government recreated the organ.

The *Águas da Ilusão* (Waters of Illusion) report (2007)[13] affirms that Celso Furtado, an expert about Northeast and the problems caused by drought in this region, have not supported the transposition of the São Francisco. In the book 'Drought and Power', he expresses his opinion on this construction:

Frente Cearense Por Uma Nova Culturada Água e Contra a Transposição das Águas do Rio São Francisco, Fortaleza, 2008. (p. 34).

11 He was economic policy secretary at the Ministry of Finance between 2003 and 2005.

12 Exame magazine, 05.25.2016, p. 60-64.

13 Transposição: águas da ilusão (2007), Magazine Transposição Final, accessed may 4, 2016 at https://psicologiadareligiao.files.wordpress.com/2007/12/revista_transposicao_web1.pdf.

I did not become interested in this project from the beginning because it was a panacea. My immediate reaction was one of caution. I always wondered: at what cost comes this investment? No one could tell me how much it would cost. Second, who will be benefiting from this? The landowners? Will they have new reservoirs to evaporate? Hope they do not resolve to start the project to get thirty years after digging an endless hole! " (Furtado, 1998 cited quote Manuelzão, 2007).

According to Henkes (2014), Celso Furtado was against the implementation of the project for «fear the risk of soil salinization in irrigated areas» so the proposal of transposition was disregarded.

The Lula government was surfing on a temporary wave of relative prosperity, which placed the country, momentary and circumstantially, in the 6th placed in the world economy ranking, without, however, raise the HDI, index which reflects the condition of life of the population. Brazil has embarked on a development project, based on consumption, with megalomaniac contours.

The state began to coordinate major investment decisions through incentives and subsidies. For this purpose, it was made use of the National Development Bank (BNDES) as a tool to strengthen a party project that did not intend to abdicate power. To deal with the international crisis at 2008, that the Brazilian government presented as a mere «small wave», the solution was to direct public banks resources to release loans to companies in certain sectors - notably the large construction companies - and, with that, make prevail the figure of Intervening State. So it increased protectionist barriers, the lending subsidized credits through public banks, especially BNDES, and the reintroduction of interventionist public policies.

Thus, the Lulism reopened national developmentalism articulating a coalition dedicated to the interests of elites, those same damned before. The Growth Acceleration Plan (PAC) would be the axis that would ensure economic growth at any cost, paid by the state, and create a development cycle - the cake that would be divided among all after the yeast worked[14]. To the economic model adopted by the

---

14 Delfim Neto, Minister of Finance in the Military Dictatorship, said it was necessary first to make the cake of the economy grow and, only then, divide it, whatever in this country actually occurred. However, the speech continues.

military regime (1964/85), the PT government adds "the illusion of implementing features based on the Asian model, inspired by the undeniable success of South Korea."[15] Of course, the plan was unsuccessful. The PAC was introduced with great splurge, touting the urgent need to accelerate growth. The PAC is a succession of plans started in 2007 and unfinished to the present. Initially, the PAC contained 16.542 projects with investments estimated in R$620 billion. Megalomania knocked the gates of the solid Petrobrás, with the construction of four refineries and shipyards that resulted in real economic disasters, such as refinery Abreu e Lima that has already reached nine times the cost initially budgeted.

According to the Trata Brazil Institute[16], basic sanitation in the country is a disaster, with more than 35 million Brazilians without access to clean water; and more than 100 million Brazilians do not have the houses connected to sewage networks. Only 40% of domestic sewage is treated, wherein in the north the number drops to 14% and in the Northeast, to 29%. Bringing sanitation for all the country would require about twenty years, at an estimated cost of 500 billion Reais. In a country, whose infrastructure is poor, with problems in almost all areas and inefficiency in services provided to the population, the government gave priority to raise dozens of stadiums, or refurbish old ones, for the 2014 World Cup, real white elephants built in Manaus, Brasilia, Natal, even wasting more money.

Many projects and works were abandoned, some for economic infeasibility, such as the Railroad East-West Integration, an expensive railroad that no has justification or a port to receive it and is paralyzed, destined to the scrapping.

Nowadays, in 2016, the investigations reveal that there were bribes in the constructions of Petrobras, nuclear power plant Angra 3, the North-South Railway, hydroelectric plant of Belo Monte and in stadiums built for the World Cup.

The PISF was designed in this context of accelerated growth and developmental constructions.

An operation codenamed "Car Wash" revealed that no work performed by PT governments is free of corruption. In the transposition

---

15 Bolívar, Folha de São Paulo, 28/8/2016
16 Accessed September, 20 2016 at http://www.tratabrasil.org.br/.

of the São Francisco River is included, OAS executives and Galvão Engenharia, which are part of the consortium responsible for two lots of land of the transposition, were arrested on suspicion of participating in a scheme to divert R$200 million from the construction.

In 2004, the work was announced as something «that neither D. Pedro II was able to accomplish», revealing the megalomaniacal tone that would guide the government›s actions and earned the president the nickname of Pedro III. At that time, the promise was to deliver the ‹Salvationist› construction in 2006. The fact is that due to the social movements and lawsuits filed to prevent their execution, the construction had only started in 2007 with estimated end at 2010. But in 2010, the project was still far from being finalized, Lula adopts another speech and ensures that its successor, Dilma Rousseff, would inaugurate the transposition in two years. In 2012, Rousseff admitted that the deadline announced underestimated the complexity of the work.

The complex construction today is estimated to end in 2017 at a cost 82%[17] higher than originally anticipated, with obvious signs of overpricing, as pointed the Federal Audit Court. Delays of this nature are not only due the lack of planning, they contribute to increase a lot the budget of the constructions and ensure that it serves as kickbacks leak.

The transposition project intends most of its the water to agribusiness (70% as total and 87% in North Axis). In this work, would come the Hydropower on the Madeira River, Angra III nuclear power station and the São Francisco River, Transnordestina and transposition of Tocantins river[18].

Even the World Bank ranked the economic model adopted by the country during the PT governments, as unsustainable. Even though acknowledging that some social inclusion was promoted, it points to the fact that 10% of the poorest population is still holding only 1% of total wealth.

---

17 Jornal Hoje (2015), Final da obra de transposição do rio São Francisco está prevista para 2007 (The end of the São Francisco river transposition is estimated for 2007), accessed on September 3rd, 2016 at http://g1.globo.com/jornal-hoje/noticia/2015/07/final- of-work-of-transpose-the-river-sao-francisco-this-expected-to-2017.html .

18 Newspaper O Estado de S. Paulo December 21, 2015.

Economic growth, when increasing the wealth of a nation, helps to increase their potential to reduce poverty and solve social problems. However, history offers numerous examples where economic growth has not brought improvement to human development. On the contrary, when growth is achieved at the expense of great inequity, high unemployment, fragile democracy, loss of cultural identity and overexploitation of natural resources, the result is the worsening of the population's lives, especially those who try to preserve traditional ways of life.

There is confusion between the terms Growth and Development, although they are often used as synonymous. This is because there is the assumption that one would end up automatically on the other. But development involves more than economic growth and structural changes. A country can grow rapidly without eliminating illiteracy or poor literacy, or improve life expectancy, or the availability of communication or increase the number of hospital and medical beds, or maintain necessary amount of calories/day, without guaranteeing access to justice and other essential services.

The classic definition of sustainable development of the *United Nations World Commission on Environment and Development* suggests a type of development that "meets the needs of the present without compromising the ability of future generations to meet their needs" (1987)[19].

To achieve this intergenerational equity, it is essential that there is, at the present, the guarantee of social equity. Because, if the economic activities of certain interest groups is endangering the welfare of other groups, we can achieve an economic growth without the occurrence of any social development.

Development cannot be measured in economic terms and ignore aspects such as changes in family structures, attitudes and mentalities, cultural change, demography, political changes, transformation of rural society and urbanization processes.

---

19 Brundtland Report, Nosso Futuro Comum (Our Common Future) (1987), accessed on August 30th, 2016 at https://ambiente.wordpress.com/2011/03/22/relatrio-brundtland-a-verso-original/ .

When governments propose development plans, even if considered sustainable and for accelerated growth, what do these proposals mean in terms of experience and the future of the planet?

> The environmental cost of growth, so far, is still insufficiently recognized (Sen 1999, p.39)[20].

Involvement and development are poles in which the dimensions of life that concerns the political level primarily and also to individual awareness of social responsibility, ethical, moral and social inclusion/exclusion are included. It is about perceiving these dimensions as dynamic polarities.

There are still companies that follow a different path from the one adopted by the West, non-industrialized societies living under the involvement tonic. According to Viana (1999, p.242)[21]

> UN-involved for the traditional populations - not only caiçara - means losing the economic, cultural, social and ecological involvement with ecosystems and their natural resources. Along with the involvement, lost dignity and the prospect of building citizenship, even knowledge is lost and with it the knowledge of traditional systems of management that, contrary to what is commonly believed, can conserve natural ecosystems more effectively than conventional technical systems. The environmental degradation process is accelerated with the expulsion - sometimes violent - of traditional populations from their lands. Obviously these consequences of development are not consistent with the pursuit of sustainability of our planet. According to Michaelis Dictionary, develop means **taking the envelope, find out what was covered; involve means to put in an envelope, to commit. Thus, we could say that developing a person or community means removing it from its housing or environmental context; disengage it with your environment. (emphasis added).**

---

20 Sen, Amartya (1999), Sobre ética e economia (About ethics and economics), São Paulo: cia letras.

21 Viana, V.M. (1999), Envolvimento sustentável e conservação das florestas brasileiras, accessed October 2nd, 2016 at http://www.scielo.br/pdf/asoc/n5/n5a21.pdf .

Thus, we must consider that these development projects reflect a particular world view, here we will try to rescue the symbolic dimensions, archetypal and mythic and discuss the various alternative of environmental socioeconomic organization.

The return to nature, according to Kaufmann (2005)[22], is one of the paradoxes of modernity.

The "Waters of Illusion" Report says no to the transposition

[...] The Government decided to follow the example of the military: to build a single great construction, which will probably never be ready, as the Transamazônica. And that even if it is finished, it will not work or solve the problem for which it construction was built for.(Waters of Illusion, p. 03)[23]

The idea to transpose a part of the São Francisco River, in order to solve the problem of drought, is not new. The first proposal to use the river to mitigate the effects of drought and the problem in Northeast comes in 1818, when the ombudsman José Raimundo dos Passos Barbosa outlined the possibility of opening a channel to take water from the São Francisco River to the river Jaguaribe (Villa, 2004 apud Henkes, 2014)[24].

During the reign of King John VI in 1820, a plan was formulated to bring the waters of São Francisco to other parts of the Northeast, at the time, only the perennial rivers, the Parnaíba and São Francisco were known. With the same old story "Too much water does not hurt, let it come," begins the construction of dams in the region.

---

22 Kauffman, Jean- Claude (2005), Casseroles, amour at crises. Ce que cuisinier veut dire, Paris: Armand Colin.

23 Transposição: águas da ilusão (2007), Magazine Transposição Final, accessed on May 4th, 2016 at https://psicologiadareligiao.files.wordpress.com/2007/12/revista_transposicao_web1.pdf .

24 Henkes, Silviana L (2014), *A política, o direito e o desenvolvimento*: um estudo sobre a transposição do rio São Francisco. .Rev. *Direito GV, São Paulo, v. 10, n. 2, p. 497-534.*

Continuing the plan that would alleviate the consequences of drought, Dom Pedro II, in 1850, commissioned a study on the river, directed by Henrique Fernando Halfeld and published in 1860 under the title "Report Atlas concerning the exploration of the São Francisco River from the waterfall of Pirapora to the Atlantic Ocean "(Villa, 2004, p.1, cited Henkes, 2014).

In October of 1877, under the impact of the drought disaster, the government of the Second Empire commissioned studies on works to mitigate the devastating effects of drought in the Northeast.

> Total mortality in the state of Ceará between 1877 and 1878, was probably close to 500,000, or more than half the population. Of these, 50,000 died from hunger and disease during the first year; 50,000 during the months of January and February 1878; during March and April, which includes the great exodus, at least 150,000 people died, mainly of hunger ... the remaining deaths came from various diseases, most linked with hunger, weakness and poor quality of food (Campos, 2014 p.70)[25].

The studies generated two types of proposals: on the one hand the dams, in the other the importation of water from perennial rivers like the São Francisco to the affected regions. But the option to transpose the waters of São Francisco, considering the financial and technological resources at that the time, was evaluated as unfeasible.

The discussion on the theme resurfaces in 1912 with the creation of the Inspectorate Federal Constructions against Drought (IOCS) again dropped in 1920 as a project infeasible due the lack of technology.

The subject left the scene for a while - although some debate remained throughout the twentieth century - and reappeared in 1981 during the military regime, to strengthen a possible candidacy of Minister Andreazza. Also at that time, the construction, summarized the transposition of 15% of the waters of São Francisco, it was

---

25   Campos, José Nilson B (2014). Secas e políticas públicas no semiárido: ideias, pensadores e períodos. *Estudos Avançados*. Vol. 28 No.82 São Paulo Oct./Dec. 2014.

considered expensive and would not serve the immediate purposes, since it would require 15 to 20 years for its construction.

In 1994, President Itamar Franco announced the opening of a bidding for the implementation of the transposition project, however, it was barred by the Federal Audit Court, that said such project would cause impact on hydro plants and irrigation in the states of Bahia and Minas Gerais.

The following year, under the Cardoso government, a basic project for the construction was designed, but was discontinued due to disagreements among the participants in the bidding process companies.

Still in Cardoso's government, in 2002, a new project was presented and archived by interference of the Minister of the Environment at that time, which advised against continuing because of the social reactions, policies and a technique that would result from the work. Until that moment and during the 2nd round of the election to the presidency, Lula and his party were standing against the work of transposition.

Once the government was reached, in 2003, Lula called for a review of the existing proposals and restart the studies to enable the transposition.

Since 2005, numerous voices from different sectors of society rose against the project, however, none had as much expression as the hunger strike of Dom Cappio, bishop from Barra, in the state of Bahia, which was a call for the revitalization of São Francisco before any construction would alter the course of the river. As the act was widely reported, the bishop was received by the President to negotiate on the revitalization and, at the time, heard many promises, ended the strike and returned to Barra.

The numerous lawsuits that blocked the start of the work were all torn down at the end of 2006, as a minister of the Federal Supreme Court (STF), Sepúlveda considered illegitimate all civil organizations that opened the proceedings. This act forever defined the fate of a river and, consequently, everything and everyone who depend on it.

Tipped the legal impediments, neutralized the opposition sectors and populations that interposed against the construction in January of

2007, it was published a permission to bid and, in March of 2007, Ibama authorized the license for the transposition installation. The army began the construction of the channels in June of the same year. Chapter III will detail the history of the struggles and battles fought on several fronts, against the construction of the transposition. Here, it is only to point out that it is a work of high impact on both the river and on the people who live around it. We understand that the reasons to do the transposition are very different from those propagated by the government are a work that has a triple function: to garner votes, ensure that by concrete channels seep the money resulting from corruption and give vent to a megalomaniac trustee whose desire to make his mark in history has no limits.

The *Águas da Ilusão* report[26] illuminates this introduction, because it brings the best and most accurate description of the facts that led to the execution of what was classified as an absurd work.

Absurd because there are more simple, efficient and inexpensive alternatives to ensure the distribution of water to the semi-arid population, as reported by the researchers from the Manuelzão Project.

For the authors, the federal government built an illusion using advertising appeals that promised land, employment and development with the arrival of water transposition. The propaganda was used not only to convince the nation that it was an essential construction, because only this would be able to bring water to the thirsty people from the backlands, but also to discredit opponents of the contract.

As often happens, many voices were raised to demystify the false advertising and reveal the true intentions of the government preventing it to make "political use of the suffering of a people without offering effective solution."[27]

The government has done everything to discredit those who opposed the transposition, although researchers, environmentalists

---

26 Estudos Avançados. vol.28 no.82 São Paulo Oct./Dec. 2014.
    Transposição: águas da ilusão (2007), Magazine Transposição Final, accessed on May 4th, 2016 at https://psicologiadareligiao.files.wordpress.com/2007/12/revista_transposicao_web1.pdf .
    Henkes, Silviana L (2014), A política, o direito e o desenvolvimento: um estudo sobre a transposição do rio São Francisco. *Rev. Direito GV, São Paulo, v. 10, n. 2, p. 497-534.*
27 Transposição: águas da Ilusão, p. 03.

and industries with great tradition in environmental studies were called the enemies of the people and the progress. Among the critics of the project were: the Brazilian Society of Limnology, the ASA: Articulation in the Brazilian Semiarid, many indigenous peoples, the Movement of Rural Workers Landless (MST), State Movement of Settlers Workers Camped and Quilombolas of Bahia, Pastoral Council of Pescadores (CPP), Pastoral of resettled, Pastoral of Youth in Popular medium (PJMP), Movement of Dam Affected People (MAB), the Pastoral Land Commission, the Lawyers Association of Brazil (OAB), Manuelzão Project of the Federal University of Minas Gerais researchers like John Abner (UFRN), João Suassuna of the Joaquim Nabuco and Aldo Rebouças Foundation, the Institute for Advanced Studies at University of São Paulo.

The government's speech was based on "without water, there is no development. " However, it is one more marketing fallacy that hides the obvious fact that the misery spreads on the margins of the abundant waters of São Francisco. Examples abound: Traipú, in Alagoas, is the city that has the 4th worst HDI of the country; Amazonian rivers, the mightiest in the world, are surrounded by poverty in Amazonian proportions.

Development, as we try to demonstrate, implies other elements that only water cannot carry, because it implies social justice, as reminds us the *Águas da Ilusão report*.

The absurd of the construction take other proportions when the own official discourse assumes that the water will not reach the scattered population of the backlands. Besides that, 26% of the water will serve as supply for cities that already have water and, finally, most of the water, 70% of the total, will be diverted to attend the agribusiness, bringing economic benefits to only certain groups.

For the authors of *Águas da Ilusão*, the work does not solve the impacts caused by drought, because the issue of drought should be managed taking into account the particularities of each place: "You have to know where a dam is required, where a cistern can resolve or where one can drill a well or collected through channels from a nearby river water. Without forgetting that the main source of water is the rain"[28].

---

28 Transposição: águas da Ilusão, p. 03.

In the semi-arid region, the rains are unevenly distributed throughout the year, but it reaches up to 800 mm/year, the same as in temperate and subtropical zones, and could be wisely managed if the political option was really «quenching the thirst» of those affected.

In addition to the social movements, many of them being the support base of Lula government's, the *Águas da Ilusão* reveals the opinion of the World Bank,[29] who refused to finance this work, because the "project has a commercial orientation" and that "international experience suggests that the link with the poor may be weak." The same judgment found that "safe supplies of water for domestic use throughout the Northeast could be secured through alternative at a fraction of the cost of the proposed project."[30]

The transposition in details

International experience has shown that the complexity of large scale projects can make them unfeasible for technical, economic, social and environmental reasons.

River's transposition projects have existed since ancient times. The Chinese, when transposed the Yellow River, became the pioneers in this experience. Mesopotamia and Egypt also built transpositions to take water from the Tigris, Euphrates and Nile to the desert regions. There are records of water transference for irrigation in Spain since the fifteenth century. We find this kind of work in South Africa, Ecuador, Peru, Spain, Mexico, USA, Canada, Libya, India, Argentina, Pakistan and other countries, always with the aim of linking surplus basins to deficit basins[31].

---

29 Azevedo, Luiz Gabriel Todt de, Porto, Rubem La Laina, Méllo Júnior, Ariosvaldo Vieira; Pereira, Juliana Garrido, Arrobas, Daniele La Porta; Noronha, Luiz Correa e Pereira (2005), *Transferência de Água entre Bacias Hidrográficas, Brasília: Banco Mundial.*.
30 Transposição: Águas da Ilusão, p. 04.
31 Neves, C. Cardoso, AP A Experiência Internacional com Projetos de Transposição de Águas: lições para o do rio São Francisco. XXIX Encontro Nacional de Engenharia de

However, not all transpositions are successful, they can create problems that compromise their effectiveness, as in the case of the shift of Colorado River waters to the Big Thompson River, after transposition, had drying up problems in the Mexican part, failures dams and introduction of pollutants in the reservoirs. The Aral Sea in Central Asia, is almost dried due to a transposition project which ignored the environmental dynamics between the rivers and irrigated fields, preventing the return of water to the affluent.

The transposition of the São Francisco has no justification, as *Águas da Ilusão* warned when quoting Alberto Daker, an expert in hydrology, irrigation and drainage. For this researcher, there are three basic conditions justifying a transposition: the existence of a basin with plenty of water remaining and land and relief that do not serve for irrigation; the existence of another basin with irrigable land, but lacking water; and have a viable cost-effective for the work to be done. In the case of the São Francisco River, none of the three conditions is contemplated: there is demand for water in farmlands near the river and there is water in the region of the receiving basin, what is not there is the guarantee of distribution. "The construction also does not hold itself energetically or financially"[32], complete Daker.

The Electric Company of São Francisco (Chesf) certifies that the Xingó and Itaparica plants operate below their capacity, because they were designed to have ten turbines each, but operate only with six. To increase energy production, it is necessary that there was more water available for new engines to work.

Produção. A Engenharia de Produção e o Desenvolvimento Sustentável: Integrando Tecnologia e Gestão. Salvador, BA, Brasil, October of 6th to 9th, 2009: <http://www.abepro.org.br/biblioteca/enegep2009_TN_STO_099_665_12814.pdf>.

32 The energy required in the water pumping is 263 MW. Adding to the 346 MW that will no longer be generated by the drop in flow along the existing hydroelectric on the lower São Francisco, the energy cost can reach 609 MW. This corresponds to more than half of all energy generated in the Sobradinho dam (1,050 MW).Available in: http://adrenaline.uol.com.br/forum/threads/a-polemica-cara-e-complexa-obra-de-transposicao-do-rio-sao-francisco-fotos.532099/ .

It is a difficult construction test, for which there was a lack of technology and the researching was happening in the same measure as the execution.

It was many years without performing great constructions in the country and today when this kind of technology is required from companies, no one has it. Government presses: the people need urgent water. And they had to get by (Jorge Kiyoshi, manager responsible for North axis work in Salgueiro, PE).

It will be 720 km of artificial channels in reinforced concrete in the two main axes of the project, according to the Environmental Impact Report of the transposition. In total, more than 2.000km of channels, including the use of dry riverbeds. The water will be captured in Pernambuco, on two points: one in Cabrobó, the North axis, and another one in Itaparica, the East Axis. These waters will need to be continuously pumped from São Francisco with high energy expenditure.

The Northern Axis will have 22 aqueducts, 6 tunnels, 26 small tanks and 4 pumping stations to bridge the gap of 165 meters. But the East Axis will have 5 aqueducts, 2 tunnels and 9 small reservoirs and 5 pumping stations that will raise the water level in 304 meters (equivalent to a building of 100 floors).

The channels are 25 meters wide and 5 meters deep, with a retreat area (in which any kind of cultivation is not allowed) of 100 meters on each side. The volume to be continuously removed from São Francisco to the transposition, granted by the National Water Agency, is 26.4 m³/s. The Government affirms that, on average, 3.5% of the river flow will be taken, and with this speech they try to convince that this is a minimum volume and that it does not affect the course of the river[33].

Águas da Ilusão brings the evaluation of Edézio Teixeria geologist to show the project unreality. According to the geologist, the maximum volume can only be removed with the following combination: the level of water in the Sobradinho dam must be above 94% of the useful volume and at the same time, receivers rivers and reservoirs must be with their levels water below the average. According to Teixeira, "statistically, these two conditions will only coincide every 12 years." Once the rainy season in Setentrional Northeast basins coincide with that of the middle basin São Francisco, which is Sobradinho, "when Sobradinho is pouring, the weirs and Northeast rivers will probably be full." In its assessment, the transposition is a waste of public money, because to make a possible use, the spending and maintenance expenses will be fixed.

He also alerts to the fact that, in some stretches, the waters from the channels would recede in no perennial rivers. In the northeast, the variation of the amount of rainfall and the volume of water that infiltrates the soil and evaporates throughout the year is very large. «It would have to be made a technical assessment to know the volume of water that is enough for the river does not dry; because otherwise the whole water to be transposed by l the channel can simply disappear.»[34]

According to experts, there is no water shortage problem in the Northeast, but a management problem. A project full of inconsistencies, which promotes environmental and social impacts, serves the very different interests of the alleged and has all the elements to feed the «drought industry».[35]

---

33 The average volume removed correspond to 17,6% of the flow that can be removed, which is 360 m3 / s, of this total, 335 m3 / s are already granted. [waters, p. 09]

34 Transposição: águas da Ilusão, p. 09.

35 Defined by journalist Marco Antonio Tavares Coelho as a "pressure for constant implementation of constructions that can mitigate the problem of

The monstrosity that is the Trans-Amazonian highway (BR-230), built by the Medici in 1970 and still unfinished, is an example of a construction that propagate benefits for those affected, but in fact strengthens the drought industry.

In addition to financial profit, there is political profit, because it transmits the image of a political/savior who performs works, brings jobs and generates development.

The electoral dividends that this kind of construction and speech brings to the government is evident. The anointed candidate, Dilma Rousseff, received in 2010, in Floresta, 86.3% of the votes; 90,7% in Cabrobó and Custódia; and 95.4% in Betânia. In the second round, Rousseff had 75% of the votes in the state of Pernambuco, the local of deviation of São Francisco river.

According to Alberto Daker, the drought industry "will be happy if enriched" with the transposition, because it needs "a construction to last for decades and decades"[36].

Apolo Heringer Lisboa warns that transposition would only be the beginning, it points for new transpositions demands, as the river Tocantins that would feed the São Francisco river: "would be the next move."[37]

Alternatives and solutions

The National Water Agency (ANA) prepared the *Atlas das Águas* (Atlas of Waters), a report containing a wide range of solutions for the urban water supply in the Northeast.

In this document, there are alternative techniques which, if implemented, would ensure the supply of water to meet the demands of the 1,300 municipalities in the northeastern semi-arid region in the nine states of the Northeast and North of Minas Gerais. The cost would reach 3.6 billion Reais, less than the 4.5 billion of the original transposition and the actual value budget of 8.2 billion. However,

---

drought, but it will not solve it, the" drought industry "aims to profit with the constructions (Transposição: Águas da Ilusão, 2007, p. 14).

36 Transposição: Águas da Ilusão, p. 14
37 Transposição: Águas da Ilusão, p. 14

these small constructions do not give visibility just like a pharaonic work, do not have the electoral appeal and do not open the floodgates to transport illicit money between construction companies and the government. It is undeniable that access to water is a basic human right. But, as shown by the authors of *Águas da Ilusão*, bad distribution of water stored in dams and perennial rivers to the scattered population of the backlands is a problem that the transposition is not intended to solve. Let>s see what is the solutions for these researchers.

For Edézio Teixeira[38], to attend the widespread demand for water an also diffused supply provider is required. The cistern is the most used technology, because it allows accumulating rainwater falling from the roofs to be used later in the dry season (June to January). The rainwater catchment can also be made by collector plates or conduction of the floods.

The Articulation in the Brazilian Semi-Arid (ASA), a forum which brings together more than 700 non-governmental entities, in July of 2003, developed the One Million Cisterns Program (P1MC), to build cisterns throughout the semiarid region.

The limitation of the tank is that the water stored (16.000 liters) is not enough for the use in agriculture, because it supplies only domestic and animals needs in the eight months of dryness.

The wells are used to take water from underground. There are more than 60,000 wells drilled in the semiarid region. Suassuna indicates that "70% of the semi-arid area has a crystalline geology that does not allow the existence of underground water, or when it does, these sources are low flow and the water is salted"[39].

According to Dilermando do Nascimento[40], this problem could be surmountable, "we need to equip the wells with desalination plants", it is necessary to invest in low-impact, but effective solution, which certainly can be improved.

Nascimento[41] also suggests the use of underground dams as "main alternative to attend the rural population of small towns with

---

38 Transposição: águas da Ilusão, p. 13.
39 Transposição: águas da Ilusão, p. 13.
40 Transposição: águas da Ilusão, p. 13.
41 Transposição: águas da Ilusão, p. 13.

population between 30 and 200 families, as regards the cultivation of family farming."

The underground dam takes the rainwater of the temporary riverbeds when they are dried, or, in the slab, as in the popular saying. For this to work, they explain[42] that we need to build a transversely waterproof wall in the riverbed to prevent water from running down in the sediment that is deposited below the surface of the river.

The *"One Land and Two Waters" Program,* also sponsored by ASA, intends to install more water infrastructure with the construction of four different structures, all with greater capacity to enable family farming: stone tanks (takes advantage of natural stone flagstones that form water deposits), underground dams, cisterns (formed by a paved gathering area, a reservoir and a small irrigation system) and clay pit trenches (deep and narrow tanks with background and wall made with stone). Luciano Silveira/ASA points out that "the program is based on the valuation of techniques already known and in the exchange of experiences between communities, in order to enhance the inventiveness of families"[43].

The suggestions proposed by the ASA were discarded. Investing huge advertising resources, the government has distorted the criticism of the project with arguments betting on ignorance and misinformation of the public, the classic example is the repeated assertion that the São Francisco river wastes (sic) the water that "throws away in the sea", and this is an affront to any student of elementary school who knows the water cycle. At the same time, the government made use of dishonest strategies with the intention to deviate from the thorny issues, in the meetings with affected communities who wanted to discuss the flooding of vast areas and the transfer of entire villages to other places, they "invented excuses which do not answer to the question we ask." (Chief Neguinho Truká).

However, advertising gimmicks do not hold up. To every liar statement, a contradiction was presented:

---

42 Transposição: águas da Ilusão, p. 13.
43 Transposição: águas da Ilusão, p. 13.

Take a pitcher of water for a northeastern person who is thirsty. (Lula, radio statement, 23/09/04).[44]

It is dishonest to say that the goal of the transposition is to quench the thirst of Ceará, Rio Grande do Norte, Paraiba and Pernambuco. The government has to say it intends to use the water from São Francisco to create new development poles based on irrigated agriculture. (João Paulo Maranhão Aguiar, engineer and adviser to the president of CHESF, 11/28/04).[45]

The *Águas da Ilusão* text denounces that this project brought land speculation, "there is a movement of companies, including multinationals, heading for the regions of the best soil in which would, in theory, be made the water transposition". (Roberto Malvezzi)[46]. The pitcher of water is perforated, the population will be left out of any possible benefit that the construction brings. About the building contractors, these will enjoy the dark waters of corruption that involve the execution of the white elephant that they are building. The government also is expected to profit and the construction would yield votes to guarantee its continuity in the state head. As the report tells us: «The population is just an extra, only the pretext"[47]. A mere pretext, but that will handle much of the loss, the other part is by the river account.

You take away the livelihood of fishermen and encourage enterprises of multinationals: the river gets less from the fish, less from the riverine and the people, and belongs more too large economic corporations and government. (Lisboa,2007)[48].

---

44 Transposição: águas da Ilusão, p. 16.
45 Transposição: águas da Ilusão, p. 16.
46 Transposição: águas da Ilusão, p. 16.
47 Transposição: águas da Ilusão, p. 16.
48 Transposição: águas da Ilusão, p. 16.

Chapter 1: The Hinterland and its history

There is all the gloom winters there, with a blazing sun and summer heat (Auguste Saint Hilaire,2003, p.141).[49]

De-Sertum, supino *de sedere,* means "what goes out of the row". The term has passed to military language, meaning the one who deserts, is not in order, disappears. The noun *desertanum* indicates an unknown place for where the deserter used to flee. The term allows the opposition between a certain and uncertain place, unknown and impenetrable ... The word, in this sense, came to Brazil in 1500, as we see in the letter of Pero Vaz de Caminha:

> De pomta a pomta he toda a praya parma mujto chaã e mujto fremosa. Pelo sertaão nos pareceu do mar mujto grande [...] (Vicenttini, 1998, p. 5).[50]

Upon the arrival of Pedro Alvares Cabral's fleet to this land, then called Brazil, remnants of complex societies such as the Mayans or Incas, for example, were not discovered. However, legends about the ruins of a lost city[51] survived until the Empire era. This town would be located between the valleys of Bahia's *caatinga,* according to the *bandeirante* known as Muribeca, who went into the hinterlands looking for silver mines. The legends about the existence of a glorious past resulted in searching expeditions during 1830s and 1840s, including the Amazon interior.

---

49 Nascimento, José Leonardo Facioli, Valentin (2003) *Juízos Críticos. Os Sertões e os olhares de sua época,,* São Paulo: Publisher Unesp..

50 A literal translation would be: From end to end, it's all beach as palm, very flat and very beautiful.The backlands appeared in, ocean view, very large [...].

51 Kuri, L. (2004), 'Homens de ciência no Brasil: impérios coloniais e circulação de informações (1780-1810)', *History, Sciences, Health* - Manguinhos, accessed on September 22nd, 2016 at http://dx.doi.org/10.1590/ S0104- 59702004000400006.

The hinterland was the area as vast as unknown until the XVIII century, but even today many consider it insurmountable due to its climate and vegetation. There is also the belief there are many hidden ghost towns there. The city narrated by that *bandeirante* conquered the Court and attracted foreign researchers. This nonexistent *sertaneja* city would have been one of the factors that encouraged the Court to lean over and study that sparsely populated region in the later years.

The first scientific expedition to the region took place in 1859. For three years, naturalists cataloged most of species near the riverbanks.

In 1871 the fame of hostile region was worsened by the drought news published by newspapers of Rio de Janeiro, capital of the Empire. It was one of the first events that deserved photos at the time. The hinterland population has never recovered from human misery.

The hinterland is in reference to the concept of misery, bandits, gangsters, blessed, fanatics, rude, crude, late, cracked earth, dusty, gnarled and thorny vegetation, dry rivers, cacti and scorching sun, dead animals skeleton, dry river ... a deserted place.

The first part of «Os Sertões»from the book *The Earth* from 1902, Euclides da Cunha became interested in the area, its geographic relief, geology, flora and fauna, in addition to endemic drought determinants of the semiarid region. He explored this unknown world and described the landscapes and local characteristics of *caatinga* resilience, as in the following quotation:

> As we have seen, when the rains come upon, the land is transfigured into fantastic mutations in contrast to the previous desolation. The dry valleys become rivers. The bare ridges are insulated and suddenly greenish. The vegetation is full of flowers, covering gaping grottos, disguising the ravines hardness and rounds in hills the collections of blocks apart - so that the great plateaus, interspersed with convales bind in smoother curves to high trays. The temperature decreases. The sunny disappearance nullifies the abnormal dryness of the air. New tones in the landscape: the transparency of space highlight the most fleeting lines in all variants of shape and color [...][52] (CUNHA, 1904, 2010, p.43)

---

52 Cunha, Euclides da (2010), *Os Sertões*, Rio de Janeiro: The Edelstein Center for Social Research.

From a traveler›s literary perspective, the hinterland appears with a geographical sense, the interior, a place far away from the coast where the country was colonized - which the *bandeirantes* sank. But it would be also a haven, a wild place with wild people. The hinterland is a kind of border between two worlds: the civilized and that one yet to civilize.

Another is the hinterland of Guimarães Rosa.Riobaldo says: «The hinterland is everywhere» (ROSA, 2001, p.24).

Rosa›s hinterland is not a geographical place anymore, it is a place with no place, mobile, not fixed, and it is everywhere. The mobile hinterland can only be the man of the hinterland who, in order to live in a place often cornered, mysterious place, has to be strong because «Hinterland is within who is strong, with cunning skills» (ROSA, 2001, p.35) [...] if God comes, he must come armed!

Even if the man leaves the geographical hinterland, it remains in him. It is the reason why the hinterland is everywhere, as Riobaldo says all the time: «The hinterland: it is within us" (ROSA, 2001, p. 325).

The Hinterlands and World Deserts

Deserts occupy 2/9 of the total planet surface but nearly 1/3 of the earth is made up of hyper-arid, arid or semi-arid zones. The Brazilian semi-arid region, as already said, was historically built from photos that inhabit both popular imagination and public policies to 'solve' the drought problem.

It is 'victimization' logic and exaltation of the limitations of natural environment that devalues all its abilities. A standard is that instead of mobilizing society for available local resources, invites to immobility, as if no one could do anything because semiarid region would be a hostile and difficult environment to develop. (Articulation in Brazilian Semi-Arid / ASA - Brazil, Luciano Silveira)[53].

---

53 Transposição: águas da Ilusão, p. 10

Unlike this logic, the Negev desert in southern Israel develops one of the most advanced agricultural systems in the world. Since the Ben-Gurion government (1948-1963), the Negev was seen as the greatest challenge to Israeli creativity. Israel is not the only example. The United States cultivates vast areas in regions like California, where it rains seven times less than in the drought Polygon[54]; even in developing countries such as Mexico, Peru, Chile and Senegal, there was a convivial learning with desert and semi-arid zones through the use of irrigated agriculture, with investment in research, education and planning. As the *Águas da Ilusão* report makes it clear, the geographical characteristics do not determine people's living conditions and should not be used politically to "justify the suffering of a population"[55].

Around eight and ten thousand years ago the current climate of semi-arid was settled and since the Empire era, the behavior of the rains has been documented[56]. Compared to other semi-arid regions of the world, which rains between 80-250 mm per year, the Brazilian semiarid region is the rainiest in the planet. It rains between 200 and 800 mm annually, with rainfall concentrated in four months and distributed unevenly.

In the semi-arid regions, the rainfall amount is usually lower than evaporation rate. In the case of Brazilian semi-arid region, this index reaches 3,000 mm per year, generating a water deficit to be managed effectively to ensure its survival and the region›s agriculture.

In the hinterland, soils are shallow, waterproof and the ground is made up of 70% crystalline rock, which favors, according to researchers, the implementation of weirs. In the semi-arid region there is already a supply of 37 billion cubic meters of water in the dams, the largest dammed volume in drought regions worldwide. Surprisingly, these dams will receive transposed water from the São Francisco River. However, there are problems with water exploitation from the dams.

---

54 The Drought Polygon comprises much of the geoeconomic Northeast Brazil and the state of Minas Gerais, that is, another name for the Brazilian semiarid region.

55 Transposição: águas da Ilusão, p. 10

56 ASA Brazil (2009), 'ASA media', accessed on January 4th, 2015 at http: //www. asabrasil.org.br/imprensa/asa-na-midia?artigo_id = 9391 .

According to Dilermando Nascimento "in large weirs on average only 20% of the potential amount stored is consumed due to a conservative management"[57].

This statement is strengthened by João Suassuna: "We don't have an effective policy for the use and distribution of this water. We could do it through pipelines and basins interconnection [...]"[58].

The ASA coordinator, Luciano Silveira, points out that among the semi-arid regions of the world, the Brazilian has the greatest biodiversity, composed by 20,000 species of animals, fungi and vegetables[59].

According to João Abner, living with the semi-arid implies the adoption of a project to effectively capture the "modest but sufficient rainwater amount"[60].

Roberto Gilson and Luciano Silveira point to the "challenge of changing the prism through which we see the semi-arid"[61]. Silveira reiterates that the transposition of São Francisco River promotes the same ineffective pattern and unsustainable development promoted in the region over the decades[62].

Furthermore, Gilson explains, the Brazilian biome, Caatinga, is *unique* on the planet:

> This is the only place where this biome exists: therefore, the caatinga is a highly adapted vegetation. What makes Northeast a minor desert is this adapted vegetation[63].

---

57 Transposição:águas da Ilusão, p. 12.
58 Transposição:águas da Ilusão, p. 12.
59 Transposição:águas da Ilusão, p. 10.
60 Transposição:águas da Ilusão, p. 11.
61 Transposição:águas da Ilusão, p. 11.
62 Transposição:águas da Ilusão, p. 11.
63 Transposição:águas da Ilusão, p. 11.

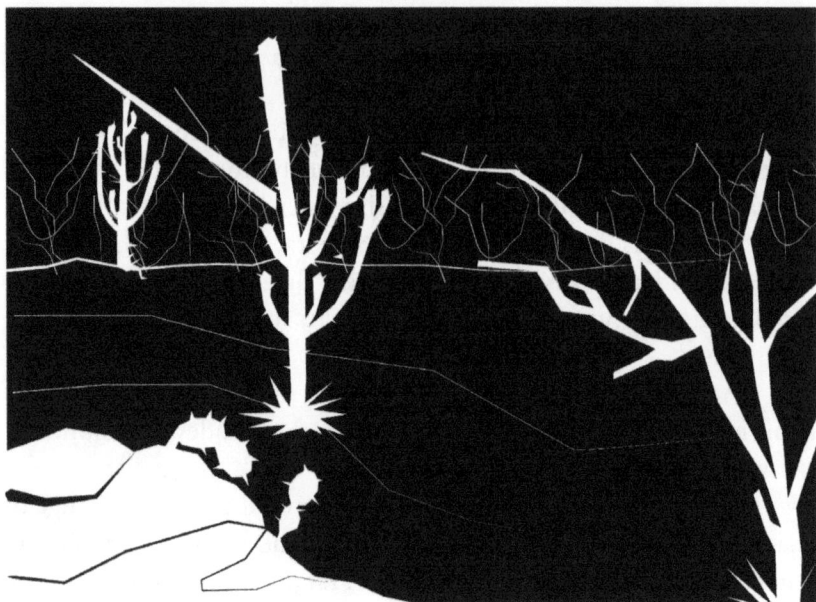

In the *caatinga* or "white forest", the landscape can change quickly. With a few drops of rain, the dry branches fill with green leafs and flowers, reissuing the scenario described by Euclides da Cunha. However, this resilience is getting smaller and it frightens researchers who warn of desertification risks in the *caatinga* due to environmental degradation.

The Northeast owns only 3% of fresh water. In Pernambuco, there are only 1320 liters of water per year per capita. The United Nations (UN) recommends a minimum of two thousand liters. According to the IPCC reports (Magrin et al., 2007)[64] and INPE (Marengo et al., 2007, Ambrizzi et al., 2007)[65], the semi-arid region tends to become more arid. The frequency and intensity of droughts will increase and the availability of water resources will decrease. This

---

64 Marengo, José A. (2008) 'Água e mudanças climáticas'. *Estud. av.* [online], 22 (63), pp.83-96 accessed on May 24th, 2016 at http://dx.doi.org/10.1590/S0103-40142008000200006.

65 Marengo, Joseph A; Noble, Carlos A; Salati, Eneas; Ambrizzi, T. (2007), *Mudanças Climáticas Globais e Efeitos sobre a Biodiversidade*. Brazil: Ministry of the Environment.

would impact on vegetation, biodiversity and activities that depend on natural resources.

Forecasts are still darker: the consequences of this change will affect feeding, hygiene and health of the local population. More than 70% of cities in the northeastern semi arid region with a population over five thousand inhabitants will suffer from water for human consumption supply crisis by 2025. About 41 million people in the semi-arid and surrounding areas will suffer from it, with the estimated growth of the population, about 1,300 municipalities of nine states in the Northeast and North of Minas Gerais.

According to experts, half of agricultural lands may be impaired, leading millions of people to hunger by the year 2050.

By 2080, maybe 400 million people will have water shortages. Northeast water tanks may receive less 70% recharge. It is the semi-arid northeast going to desertification[66].

Rainwaters are stored by plants and consumed during dry season. The nutrients remain stocked in roots, while plants lose leaves to reduce water loss through transpiration. The hinterland dweller knows the function and utility of each species as well as researchers. The government ignores it, being unable to carry out effective policies to ensure the distribution and use of existing water and create innovative alternatives as well as to educate for its correct use. Although most of the rivers in the region are not perennial, they are polluted and bear the consequences of the lack of basic sanitation.

The *caatinga* originally covered an area of 1 million square kilometers. Currently, the remaining area is 734,478 km2, with less than 1% under the protection of conservation units. Deforestation for firewood removal is one of the main activities that contribute to desertification, drought and loss of Brazilian biodiversity.

Caatinga has 45% of deforested area and the third most degraded biome in the country after the Atlantic Forest and Cerrado. The *caatinga* has fundamental importance to the planet's biodiversity, since 1/3 of its plants and 15% of its animals are endemic species. In

---

66 Marengo, José A. (2008) Água e mudanças climáticas'. *Estud. av.* [online], 22 (63), pp.83-96 Accessed on May 24th, 2016 at http://dx.doi.org/10.1590/S0103-40142008000200006.

this peculiar region, the political institutions and their manipulative tactics, used and abused the climatic condition to justify the misery of the hinterland and its people, concealing the real reasons of its unworthy life for decades. It was expected that the government with a "popular democratic vision for the working class", as they like to be classified, were expected to demystify and face the question of semiarid region, promoting conditions to develop a living culture with drought, supporting actions such as those that ASA has been promoting for years. But it was not the government policy option, since they took the same speech of the old colonels to justify their absurd and useless pharaonic work to the semiarid and which is known to leave out the diffuse populations.

> Poverty is due to lack of policies. The US, Israel and Chile did not throw its population in poverty. The semiarid region is feasible, does not suit the existing misery in Brazil [...] there is a certain difference in treatment that was given to these semiarid and our semiarid region. It is different, but exemplary: access to education, research development, physical infrastructure and transport make up a set of measures that make a difference. (Gilson Roberto Campos, National Council of the *Caatinga* Biosphere Reserve)[67].

In the semiarid, there was always a large concentration of land, water and resources in the hands of a dominant minority and coronelism that has not been fully extinguished in these country corners yet. Social exclusion and environmental degradation are critical determinants of social and environmental situation in the region.

Data about the region reveals that about 1.5 million farmers (28.82% of total Brazilian family farms) occupy 4.2% of arable land in the semiarid region. Only 1.3% of farm settlements with more than 1 000 hectares, known as *latifundia* (plantiation or large estate), holds 38% of the land. It is an absurd level of concentration that produces immense social inequality.

Among the Brazilians in extreme poverty, more than a half (59.1%) lives in the Northeast region. Among these, 52.5% live in rural areas (IBGE, 2010), most of them in semiarid region. 60.09% of the municipalities in the semiarid region (corresponding to 9

67 Transposição:águas da Ilusão, p. 10.

million people), the Human Development Index (HDI) ranges from Very Low and Low, which demonstrates a poor indicator of longevity, education and income. All municipalities in the semiarid region showed HDI lower than Brazil (0.727).

According to IBGE[68] (Population Census 2000), half of the population in the semiarid region has no income or their only income comes from government benefits, 59.5% are women. Those who receive a minimum wage are approximately five million people (31.4%), of which 47% are women. Only 5.5% have income between two and five minimum wages, 67% of them are men and out of 0.15% with incomes above 30 minimum wages only 18% are women.

The Gini index measures the level of inequality from income. It is above 0.60 for more than 32% of municipalities in the semiarid region, which confirms the extreme concentration of income.

Truká and Pipipá people, characters from the next chapter are living in this natural and policy setting, however in a different way. Truká's territory is next to the Old Chico; most of these people live in Assunção Island and other river islands. Before the transposition, Pipipás' territory was many kilometers from São Francisco, but currently, part of their land entered long straight with the river as the eastern axis cross one of their villages, the Caraíbas.

There is another important element to say which has weight in the comparison of the both situations: the Truká have their demarcated territory, since the Pipipá have only a recognized territory. This is an important political and legal issue: the demarcation ensures a number of Brazilian government bonds in relation to Truká, since only the recognition does not. During the Dilma government (2011-2016), the demarcation processes were paralyzed. And in the case of transposition, the government ignored its constitutional obligations in relation to indigenous peoples even with demarcated lands. According to Pipipá, the picture is more gloomy: as mere recognition does not bring legal obligations to the state, there is no bargain and when there is a dialogue with the technicians in charge of the work, they say everything seems to be vague, neither the chief nor other leaders seem aware of what will happen when the work is finished.

---

68 Accessed may 28th 2016 at http://www.ibge.gov.br/home/.

The São Francisco Basin

The watershed of São Francisco River[69] covers 639,219 km2 of drainage area (7.5% of the country) and average flow of 2,850 m3 / s (2% of the country). The São Francisco River is 2,700 kilometers long and rises in the Serra da Canastra, Minas Gerais. It runs south to north through Bahia and Pernambuco, where its course changes eastwards, reaching the Atlantic Ocean on the border between Alagoas and Sergipe. The basin is present in seven Brazilian states: Minas Gerais (36.8%), Bahia (48.2%), Pernambuco (10.9%), Alagoas (2.2%), Sergipe (1.2%), Goiás (0.5%) and Federal District (0.2%). It covers 507 municipalities (about 9% of the country's municipalities).

In order to plan and facilitate the location of its large population and natural environment and taking into account the large size of the basin, a division according to the course of São Francisco and its altitude variation was made. Thus, from Serra da Canastra to Pirapora city, in north-central Minas Gerais, was named Alto São Francisco, which owns 1280 kilometers above sea level and an area of 111,804 square kilometers.

In the south-north direction, the Old Chico runs through the west of Bahia to the point where it was formed the dammed lake of Sobradinho, in the Remanso municipality. This stretch is called Middle São Francisco, reaching 339,763 km2.

In the next stretch, the river changes its course to the east, creating a natural border between the states of Bahia and Pernambuco until reaching the border with Alagoas. It's the São Francisco Submedium with 155,637 km2.

Still continues eastward, again as a border between two states: Alagoas and Sergipe. It is the Low São Francisco, an area of 32 013 km2, where the São Francisco River flows into the Atlantic Ocean.

The São Francisco Basin constitutes fragments of different biomes: Atlantic forest, *cerrado, caatinga*, coastal and island.

---

69   Information on the São Francisco River Basin extracted from: http://cbhsaofrancisco.org.br/a-bacia/.

The socio-economic reality of the São Francisco River basin presents great contrasts, reflecting thus largely inequality that still characterizes Brazilian society.

Specifically in the economic sphere, there is a strong presence of industries and agribusinesses between regions, as in the Upper, Middle and Sub-middle: industrial mining zones and agroindustrial poles of grains and fruit located in the north and west of Bahia and in the south of Pernambuco. In the course of the Low, the riverine economy still binds to traditional farming and fishing, however, there is a significant growth of aquaculture, tourism and leisure.

The São Francisco River yesterday and today

For indigenous people who live around the river, it is vitally important and is not conceived as a mere natural resource, but a relational entity whom they bow to. For them, the São Francisco was *Opará* (river-sea) part of its symbolism and life. The Portuguese civilization was already established, natives subjugated through genocide, catechizing and slavery, *Opará* became São Francisco officially, which also for its importance in life, is called by its riverine populations, as mestizo, *Old Chico*, an affectionate way of referring to the river. Old

Chico, due to its beauty and strength, is sung in verse and prose by music and popular literature.

Especially since the last century to the present day, the Old Chico has been mistreated intensely as to be able to say that it reached the twenty-first century as a dying river. But it was not always so. Not by literature look of naturalists of the nineteenth century. They were based on Alexander von Humboldt, the idea of experiencing nature and Goethe›s idea, who understood nature as a large living organism that would never be exhausted. That nineteenth-century literature used to list data about flora, fauna, climate, culture, everyday life and topography.

Saint-Hilaire, a member of the special mission of the Duke of Luxembourg, traveled through the São Francisco River basin, had an optimistic view. At one point of his records, he says that the interior will meet new features and «It will always remain to him as thick pastures, fertile land, and a navigable river in immense extent, established as useful for communications between the country and the ocean «(Saint-Hilaire, 1938, p. 278).

Among detailed records about the hospitality and generosity of riverine and many others about excessive heat and uncomfortable accommodation, it reserves considerable space to talk about trade along São Francisco. Cotton, for instance, could be exported to «Pernambuco and Bahia by the river, and beans as well as corn can be interchanged by brought salt from the saline region, located on the river bank, and where excessive drought opposes cultivation cereals «(Saint-Hilaire, 1938, p.320). Sugar and moonshine produced in Salgado-BA were commonly exchanged for salt. Prosperity, according to the writer, reigned among the inhabitants of the city due to exchange trade of wealth achieved in the river.

Johann von Spix and Carl Martius, members of "Austrian mission", were aligned to the Grand Duchess Leopoldina of Austria, who came to settle in Brazil and became empress by marriage agreement with D. Pedro I. As Saint-Hilaire, these two naturalists jointly produced reports on the salt production and salt trade marketplace with Minas Gerais traders as well as the order of the product throughout the countryside by São Francisco river.

Many pages were devoted to life on the river. Reports show an increasingly distant reality from its current situation. They were impressed with the quantity and quality of what they saw: species of fantastic animals, such as various types of bats inhabiting Minas Gerais, especially the regions of the caves on the bank of the river São Francisco. The meat farm by the edge of a large pond formed by this river, two naturalists were "transported to an entirely diverse country. They were verdant forests, which bordered extensive fishy lagoons "(Spix & Martius, 1981, p. 96). In general, naturalists held a relation based on enchantment and awe for nature. They used to relate the "civilizing activity" with destruction.

Time passed and developmental and predatory impulses prevailed. Currently in the Old Chico there are hydroelectric complexes: Three Marias, Sobradinho, Itaparica, Paulo Afonso Complex I, II, III, and IV and the Xingó. The dams, in addition to changing the life of the river, were responsible for violent process of eviction of people from the regions where they are located. There is still construction forecast of several dams and other hydroelectric projects in the river[70].

There are many fronts of big business, highly profitable; attacking the existence of the river and the lives it sustains[71]. One such business is the agro-fuel or customarily called biofuel, a name that conceals what it really is: the production of ethanol is by large monoculture of sugarcane. A total of 510,000 hectares only in the state of Bahia, is used for sugar cane cultivations. It also means that, on average, it takes 510,000 liters of water for irrigation, or in other words, it takes 3600 liters of water to make 1 liter of ethanol[72]. Monoculture of sugarcane has also meant illegal deforestation, attack on biodiversity, forest fires and pollution because of the cane straw, water contam-

70 CIMI data reporting Report (2007), 'Indigenous people affected with the transposition of the São Francisco River, accessed on September 15th, at http://www.cimi.org.br/pub/publicacoes/1241549933_relatapoinmetransp.pdf.

71 Report-complaint 'growth acceleration in the São Francisco River Basin: the stroke of conflicts and social and environmental injustices' (2008), accessed on May 20th, 2015 at http://docplayer.com.br/7108933-Aceleracao- of the growth-in-bowl-of-river-sao-francisco-the-Path-of-conflict-and-social injustices-and-ambientais.html

72 idem.

ination by manure and pesticides, ponds destruction affecting fish reproduction.

Irrigation is today the largest consumer of the basin waters. It is expected that in a short time, the demand for water will be 648 thousand liters per second to 640,000 ha. Two of the tributaries of São Francisco River are at their limit: Corrente and Grande rivers, both in Bahia.

There are also the mining and steel industry issues, concentrated in the Upper and Middle São Francisco: Minas Gerais and Bahia. The removal of minerals suppresses vegetation, soils are removed, phreatic zones are lowered, causing pollution, erosion and siltation, while the steel industry heavily relies on charcoal. And to obtain this material, there is illegal deforestation, implementation of large monocultures, particularly eucalyptus, besides living with complaints of using child and adult slave labor. The eucalyptus plantation has created real green deserts and evicted entire communities from their lands.

In the medium São Francisco, in the municipality of Caetité-BA, there is uranium exploitation and it has polluted the water. Analysis shows 7 times higher radioactivity levels than the parameters established by the World Health Organization.

Lack of basic sanitation standards is another adverse circumstance affecting the river from its source region. Domestic sewage falls directly into the waterways of the rivers basin, and when they receive treatment, it is only primary.

Another predatory activity is fish farming. The Valley Development Company of the São Francisco and Parnaíba (Codevasf), state-owned enterprise under the Ministry of Integration (MI), is supporting the creation of aquaculture centers by Minas Gerais, Bahia, Sergipe, Alagoas and Pernambuco. It is an activity that contaminates and kills other species of commercial fish in São Francisco. So, in 2015 and 2016 the repopulation of native fish in the Old Chico was necessary. The fingerlings were produced by the CODEVASF and thrown into the river[73].

---

73 Ministry of Infrastructure (2016), 'Rio São Francisco received 1.9 million native fish in 2015' (2016), accessed on February 14th, 2016 at http://www. brasil.gov.br/infraestrutura/2016 / 02 / rio-sao-francisco-received-1-9- a million-to-fish-natives in 2015 .

The report-complaint *Aceleração do Crescimento na Bacia do São Francisco* (Growth Acceleration in the São Francisco Basin) of 2008, states that four nuclear power plants on the São Francisco banks were planned to be built. The risks associated to this type of plant are large and well known. If these provisions were complied, the country is taking a stance against countries such as Germany, Switzerland, Italy, Belgium and Sweden, who reviewed its energy policy and decided to shut down nuclear power plants.

In the report-complaint mentioned above, the list of large domestic and foreign capital companies[74] placed in this appalling environmental setting is great and serves state and federal governments interests that are seen as complicit by the same report.

With so many attacks, the Old Chico is dying and the signs are visible. For the first time, in 2014, the source of this beautiful and important river, located in the Serra da Canastra National Park, Minas Gerais, simply dried up.

In opposition to the version published by environmental agencies and media, which blamed the prolonged drought (three years), in an interview[75], the president of São Francisco River Basin Committee sees large-scale change in the local ecosystem: "[...] Three Marias and Sobradinho are being threatened and approaching the useful volume limit of water. In other words, water in the main tributaries is coming to zero level. And the river's biodiversity is committed beyond its deteriorating quality."

When in an interview[76], José Alves Siqueira was asked about the role of prolonged drought in the Northeast in the river extinction process, he answered: "It's one more aggravating issue due to increas-

---

74 Companies mentioned in the report are: Agricultural Xingu group, Multigrain arm; Louis Dreyfus Commodities and Total, already cited in the text; Korean Celltrion; Japan's Itochu Group; Brazilian Petrobras, Votorantim and Odebrecht; Toledo group, Codevasf, real estate developers and private banks as St. Andrew Bank, FNP, CODEVERDE and Lafico; the Valourec Manesmann.

75 Aleixo, Caroline, Portillo, Carolina (2014), 'Director Park said that the main source of the São Francisco River dried', accessed 20 semtember 2015 at http://g1.globo.com/mg/centro-oeste/ news / 2014/09 / director-de-park-said that main-spring-from the-river-sao-francisco-secou.html

76 Primeira Edição (2012), 'San Francisco can be extindo says biologist', accessed April 2nd, 2015 at http://primeiraedicao.com.br/noticia/2012/12/26/sao-francisco-pode-ser -extinto-said biologist.

ing water demand. The sandbars in São Francisco are increasing. We are living a process of global warming and the *caatinga* is the most susceptible Brazilian place for climate change".

According to FUNAI (National Indian Foundation) reports, cited in the Impact Report, the effects of Sobradinho on Indians Basin are worrying, especially regarding the volume of water, supply of fishes and quality of water reported by Truká as yellowish and strong smelling during the winter.

Siqueira and 99 other researchers warn the inexorable process of extinction of the river[77]. They claim that today there are only four percent of vegetation on its banks. The lack of green cover accelerates erosion and river siltation. Soils with high levels of salinity and water from reservoirs become brackish. Thus, desertification areas tend to increase. Old Chico is unfeasible as waterway due to silting, accumulation of rubble, trash and debris that interfere in the topography of the riverbed, reducing its depth and making time stand less water, causing flooding in the rainy season. This is one of the river death causes.

Regarding the ongoing transposition in the river extinction process, Sequeira says: "We still don't have clear answers. We found 62 invasive quaint species into canal areas, which are not from Brazilian flora. When it [the invasive] arrives, it will take up space of native species and causes destruction of the other"[78].

Even with this discouraged scenario, the researcher believes in the possibility of mitigating impacts, however, by his own words, it is impossible to feed any hope:

> Something to be done on an emergency basis [is] the implementation of degraded areas recovery program. Large contractors are required to implement these recovery plans. This is not happening. When they offer the possibility, it is made with invasive exotic species. We have a set of opportunities that cannot lose sight. We will not have a second chance. There is no sensationalist meaning about it. It is not a free criticism.[79]

---

77 Idem.
78 Idem.
79 Idem.

Chapter II: The Land of Women, Men and the Magical Creatures

In the second part of Os Sertões, Euclides da Cunha researched its population and miscegenation in order to understand the genealogy of the Hinterland man.

For him, the *Sertanejo* (Hinterland man) is a country man, another kind of man ascribed to rustic customs and lifestyle, opposed to the city man who lives in the urban and industrial process.

> The *Sertanejo* is, above all, strong. They don't suffer from exhausting rickets like the neurasthenic mestizos of the coast do. 35. 90 A drought doesn't cause them to panic. It is a complement to their stormy life, forging it in tremendous scenarios (Cunha, 2001, p.207)[80].

Cunha is seeking the roots of a new society, an authentic national civilization whose mother was nature itself. Adopting the views of determinism to provide explanations of the Hinterland's reality, the author suggests that the Hinterland man was "closer to nature", therefore it would be a more pure and more the authentic expression of national identity.

According to the author, what would distinguish the Hinterland would be its isolation, which promoted the assimilation of nature's features that surrounded it, as well as the conservation of old and remote traditions of indigenous ancestors.

It is worth noting that the Brazil Euclides da Cunha lived in the transition to the twentieth century, which inspired him to perform a civilizing mission. For him, despite the hinterland people being the bearers of the authentic national identity, it would have to assimilate to its nation, break their isolation, change their customs, in fewer words, civilize it, which meant conforming the model of the urban man.

---

80 Cunha, Euclides (2001), Os Sertões.São Paulo, Editorial Atelier

But, being a man of the Hinterlands, an interbred mestizo, was seen as someone who needs to be incorporated into its nation, which can be said about the Hinterland man living in the mainland and who keeps, to date, the specifics of their ethnicity, their culture and their lifestyle ignored by the steamroller progress speech.

Cunha thought the Hinterland man as the only model to inhabit the Hinterlands, however, this is not true. The Hinterlands, are inhabited by native settlers who are in process of rescuing their identity and prevent it from fading, despite more than 300 years of colonization.

As announced, we intend to bring into scene the most affected characters by the work of the transposition so they can provide their statements, express their views and opinions on the impact of a work that modifies its environment and, to some extent, its lifestyle.

Who are they? A bit of history about the Truká people

Since the beginning of colonization of the Brazilian territories, the mainland was an object of interest for the Portuguese for occupational purposes. From the coastline to the Hinterland, the colonizers found other people who lived there and, with them, were confronted in different ways, enslaving, exploiting their labor, waging wars and wiping out entire ethnic groups, when they were not exterminating their indigenous identity to confine them into Catholic settlements.

In 1556, Mem de Sá (second general-governor of the Brazil Colony) established missions, initially on the coast and then heading inland through the "slave raids"[81]. The Hinterlands would be occupied by the colonizers for livestock in order to provide meat and animal traction power to sugar mills installed in the coastal region. The colonial hinterland occupation came across the São Francisco river and was marked by the exploitation of livestock and training of indigenous settlements around missionary activities by the Jesuits,

---

81 The slave raids were expeditions, in principle, not military, made by missionaries to convince the Indians that *come down* from their villages to live in new settlements specially created for this purpose in the vicinity of colonial settlements.

Franciscans and Capuchins (Monteiro, 2008; Batista, 2005; Pompa, 2002; Moura, 1993; Andrade Belt, 1984; Pierson, 1972).

If the coast is reserved for planting sugarcane and processing in the mills, the hinterland supplies meat and sometimes indigenous slave labor, leaving the middle region of the São Francisco River, marked by intense conflicts between «Curraleiros» and missionaries around the villages.

According to some historians, Martins de Nantes was responsible for the formation of the Rodelas Mission, in 1679. At that time, it is said that an Indian codenamed Rodelas would have fought alongside the Portuguese in the expulsion of the Dutch and therefore gained fame and protection. The village was installed in the Middle region of São Francisco, in the Parish of Our Lady of Conception of Rodela (Batista, 2005), where the Tapuias-Cariris or Cariris (Pompa, 2002) were located. Now known as Pambu Island, where the Truká (Pernambuco) and Tumbalalá (Bahia) currently live.

The ethnic groups that occupied the region were submitted, or even massacred, the remaining descendants of these groups, in the past century, reclaimed, or fought to rescue their identities and their lands. In addition to Truká and Tumbalalá, the Tuxá, Pankará, Atikum, Pipipã, Pankararu and Xucuru, among others, inhabit the basin of the São Francisco River. Mainly descendants of Cariris, who had a similar story of submissions, of newer settlements and resurgences.

Standing out in this scenario is the colonizer Garcia D›Avila, an official of the Portuguese crown in Brazil, considered a reliable man, and legitimate son of Thomas de Souza (first general-governor). From the lands received in the colony, enriched by livestock and other commercial activities, creating perhaps the largest estate in the history of Brazil called the Tower House. The Tower House dominated the Brazilian Hinterlands for decades, including the São Francisco mid region, and was the protagonist of conflicts between missionaries and indigenous populations of the region.(OPIT, 2007; Calmon, sd).

According to Batista, "Assunção village" probably was founded around 1722, the island was formerly known as Pambu, after missionary orders, elevated the village in 1761. The village had many of its buildings destroyed by a flood in 1792. It was inhabited by indigenous families: a reasonable number of people were living from fishing, hunting and land cultivation (Young, 1817 apud Baptist, 2005). With the decline of breeding and cattle trade in the region, there seems to have been a decrease of colonizing pressure on its inhabitants, allowing a period of autonomy in the villages. However, the pombalinos decrees of 1755 are worth mentioning, which sought to integrate Indians into Brazilian society, allowing marriage between Indians and non-Indians and administrating their land by themselves, culminating in the extinction of the missionary orders in Brazil (OPIT, 2007 and Batista, 2005).

Between the 1850s and 1870s, correspondence between the Mayor of Assunção Village and the Board of Indians indicate the occurrence of conflicts involving indigenous lands and the "powerful hinterlands", warning of the need to demarcate their territory [82]. According to the memory of the current residents of Assunção Island, the first Mayor of the village would have been Captain Bernardino, key figure for the Truká people in the reconstruction of their ethnic identity. The period of the Brazilian Empire was marked by land conflicts in the region between Indians and non-Indians, having an unfavorable position the State in relation of the rights of the first aforementioned (OPIT, 2007).

The twentieth century would be subject to various interferences with the issue of ownership and use of the lands. In 1920, the Bishop of Pesqueira, stated that the lands of the Assunção Island would have been donated to the saint Our Lady of the Assunção and belonged to the Church and therefore they sold them to farmers in the region and then came to collect taxes for their use (Batista, 2005 and OPIT, 2007).

Later, there were state-owned enterprises with development projects such as the construction of several dams along the São Francisco River course. In the midst of these development projects, a vision that nature is a source of resources to be exploited for the capitalist economy statement remains, which invariably causes the dispersion of traditional communities or their impoverishment (Fischer, 1999 Waldman, 2005 and Monteiro, 2008).

---

82 Batista, Mercia Rejane Rangel (2005), *Descobrindo e recebendo heranças: as lideranças Truká,, 2005. 265 f. Thesis (Doctorate in Anthropology) - Graduate Program in Social Anthropology, National Museum of the Federal University of Rio de Janeiro - UFRJ, Rio de Janeiro.*

By the São Francisco River, since 1950, the Three Marias, Sobradinho, Itaparica, Moxotó, Paulo Afonso and finally Xingó (1990 decade) dams were built. The construction of the hydroelectric plant Luiz Gonzaga, popularly known as Itaparica, resulted in the dispersal of more than 200 indigenous families of the ethnic group Tuxá and traditional riverside dwellers of the São Francisco River, in the state of Bahia (Monteiro, 2008; Scott, 2009).

As part of the state actions on the exploration and use of indigenous lands in the region, it is still possible to refer to the governmentˌs project of Pernambuco which was installed in the year 1965, the Company Reseller and Colonization - *Companhia de Revenda e Colonização*, (INCRA), to provide land and finance agricultural production for farmers in the region. With the end of that company, the government would set up on the island Cia seedlings production and Selected Seeds of Pernambuco - *Cia de Produção de Mudas e Sementes Selecionadas do Estado de Pernambuco* (SEMEMPE), turning the land into large seedling production fields, generating significant environmental impacts and conflicts with the ancient inhabitants of island (Monteiro, 2008 OPIT, 2007; Batista, 2005).

In 1967 the National Assistance Indian Foundation (FUNAI) was created, which replaced the former Indian Protection Service (SPI). This foundation, however, until 1987, worked in the area sporadically, along the gradual process of liberation of the land of SEMEMPE. According to Batista (2005), their performance was done in an unorganized manner, generating conflicts in the redistribution of land on the island. For the Organization of Indigenous Teachers Truká (OPIT), there was great interference in the way traditional Truká organization was done «imposing a culture of hierarchy, overlapping the social organization of the people» (OPIT, 2007, p.30). FUNAI would have created the Tribal Council, following two criteria: being older, being male and acted in choosing a new Chief. According to the OPIT:

> The idea of organization imposed by FUNAI did not follow the same logic of social organization that our people had, as our leaders were chosen by nature, according to the following guidelines: belong to traditional families; participate of Toré privately; must be approved by the Charms. (OPIT, 2007: 31).

Amid the conflicts over land and the interference of the state and its policies for development and protection/subjugation of indigenous peoples, Truká developed a history of struggle, resistance and negotiations. In ancient times, the story of Francisco Rodelas (probably belonging to Tuxá people, neighbor of the Truká) can be remembered, who won the title of captain; also in the nineteenth century, Mayor Captain Bernardino efforts during the first decades of the twentieth century, partakes the land struggle movement, inspired by revelations of Charms and action of various leaders.

Among Truká, Acilon Ciriaco, perhaps, were the most important leaderships in the recent process of struggle for lands and identity recognition of the indigenous people. Mayor Bernardino's health declined, as he underwent serious physical and mental issues. Thanks to the work of the Tuxá women with the Particular and with the Toré, it was revealed to him that he would be healed to fulfill the mission of "discovering the village." Between the 1930s and 1940s, he worked extensively with the Particular and with Toré in the development process of revealing Charms, that were teaching about their own people the Truká and their "science." The Charms revelations (ancestral spirits) through the Toré and through dreams, allowed Acilon and his companions, as Antonio Cirilo, start a new chapter of struggle for the reconquest of their lands in Assunção Island. Even with all effort, not just religious, but political, as demanded several times regulation to the SPI, they still would not get possession of the land.

The final possession of the land would only come in the 1990s and the entire island of Assunção in 2002, after several actions organized by Truká known as the "recovery". The "recoveries" are portions of land that have been reoccupied, originally belonging to the indigenous people, in order to pressure legislation to their advantage. The "recoveries" are tactics that do not serve to claim the lands, but also reaffirm their ethnic identity. Between 1981 and 2007, five "recoveries" were performed. The last "recovery", in 2007, in the Antonio Lalinha farm, in the town of Cabrobó, is directly related to the transposition of the São Francisco River, when their position opposed the government's imposition of doing this project.

In recent events, impactful projects of the government and the continuity of the struggle through the "recoveries" are indicators that the history of the struggle for lands, for political recognition, rights and autonomy of the indigenous Truká people since colonial times, has evolved and re-edited in the imposition development projects, the promotion of regional conflicts between Indian and non-Indian's will is the resistance of a population that insists on living accordingly to their traditions.

The Truká today

The first contact with the Truká people, in February 2013, was by Claudia Truká, indigenous teacher and leader, at the time, of the theater group composed of young people of the tribe. All interviews were conducted between February 2013 and July 2015.

From the beginning, the effort was evident, especially from indigenous leaders, to contribute to the strengthening of the people and identity through political action. In their struggle, the transposition of the river was an important issue, which had been going on since 2007.

With a population of about 4,000 Indians distributed in 25 villages, you can see the group, differences, disagreements, conflicts and diversity. Among young people, some express a desire to have more diverse professions - such as actresses, doctors, social workers, singers, teachers, or just get a job in one of fields in order to work with a formal contract. There are those who wish to conquer the world, while others want to stay on the island, get married, have children and raise a family. Some are Catholics, others are more attached to the rituals with the Charmed. There are some more politically engaged in social movements, others are more busy with work in the fields. Some live close to the city of Cabrobó, attend Salgueiro college, while others work in the banana plantations, rice, onions and build houses for families that are starting. These differences highlight the complexity of Truká society, living among the modern and the traditional, conservative and its transformations. The coexistence of the rural world is permeated by the urban world, worlds that are not separated but connected by information networks, that impact on lifestyles and promote cultural change while demonstrating value and rescue the traditional cultural values. It is observed that there is a selectivity about which values and practices would be rescued because the intention is not to return to the eighteenth century, or to abdicate achievements acquired with modernity. The Truká make use of traditional medicine, while maintaining health centers in the villages and a hospital exclusively for indigenous people in Cabrobó. The complexity of social, economic and gender are present in this indigenous society, is part of a process of identity affirmation and the struggle for rights beforehand mainstream society that often opposes the interests of these traditional populations.

Transpositionning the voice of Truká

For Truká, the Old Chico is life and ancestry. Therefore, expectations about what will happen to the transposition bring a lot of trouble. As noted in the fervent testimony of a shaman:

> Because the transposition through the Truká territory goes far as it can, everything will be immersed with it. Are we the ones that

are going to work there? No, they do not allow us. There are other people that will be put there. I mean, to the governments interest. And young people at that time, should have joined, "we will retake this land. you can give where you gave. " (Pajé Adilson).

No wonder, the impacts of the project were and are immense:

[...] Because there the foot hacksaw was degraded the forest that had to build there. It has begun. They say "no, it will not have an impact," but a stone that we take from a site already changed its nature. If you take a stone from one place and put on the other, nature is being modified. And for us, what else really hurts is to know that in addition to destroying nature, the poor will not benefit from this water, which is the worst. [...] At the time that the army came, the number of prostitution, according to the health department, and the number of sexually transmitted diseases increased sharply because people came from all over the country, everywhere people came to work. And the issue of drugs also rose sharply, the reason why I'm skeptical. Our young people who went to work in the implementation knew people who were users and, as a consequence, began to experiment. It entails that we already have people here that are also users. And all this because of the transposition, indirectly because it. (Chief Bertinho).

The Chief Neguinho, from Caatiguinha Village, reports the expectations and what actually would have happened:

The city, the perspective that we have is none, because everyone, almost 90% of whom were small farmers who went to transpose cannot afford to go back to the fields. There is no way back, there is no incentive for any families to farm here. People who were in the channel band they thought they would receive millions in compensation, many people are disappointed with one hand on the barrel and another closing, why? All lands that cross the channel, here on the banks of Cabrobó, are indigenous lands, no one has a deed to the land. So the government has to channel strip and the guy had a property of 50 ha. So, the guy was there to receive the compensation that came to him, just to regularize he spends more than ... So thus took these people, some of these people for productive villages they did, the confined people being supplied by water tanker trucks, most homes these productive villages are abandoned. (Chief Neguinho).

And Chief Neguinho still remains skeptical for any hope:

How many people have hope that the water will reach them. Because, in fact, you now have the Pecém channel, in Ceará, and people cannot get water inside. It is patrolled 24 hours a day and patrolled with a sky jet. Then, the transposition project, from our point of view, the way it is going to be is just another agricultural business, it will be for large companies, which are already in Suape, in the Port of Pecem waiting. Suape will sustain while the other companies are there waiting to produce. That is our concern, no, let's see if we can now ensure that in fact it is to quench the thirst ...

Ana Maria, teacher, member of the theater group, saw the work as a point of no return:

Almost no one speaks about it, right? In transposition. For today, I see that is a work in vain, because we fought, and claimed nothing was done. They promised they would revitalize the river and to till today, nothing yet! Only digging there, inside of Caatinga, degrading, is not it? The environment means nothing! Nothing good for the city, for the community, for the people. THERE WAS NOTHING. (Ana Maria).

By the year 2014, nor the mitigation policies seemed to quench the disbelief in the work wich can be seen in the testimony of Claudia Truká, indigenous teacher:

When you start the work of transposition, Ciro Gomes comes to visit the territory at the time he was the minister of Integration, so when Ciro Gomes came to our people, and then teachers, communities, leaders, there in those sheds tell Ciro Gomes ... [...] so they can hear loud and clear that the transposition project, because he came to inaugurate the road and some houses that we had won, then there Neguinho told him clearly with one voice , who was the voice of the people, the asphalt and the houses do not, in any way, buy us, we were against the transposition and were going to do whatever it takes so that it did not happen, to recover our territory, then he does not I think this would be an exchange, a currency trading, it would not be a bargaining chip ... (Claudia Truká).

The opinion of young people on the river transposition project is essential to understand the meanings impacts and reactions, to understand how the Truká seek to rebuild their culture and cosmology and how, in the face of a threat to the environment, they can articulate their political struggle.

Maurilio is a young teacher, who went to college in Salgueiro, and the leader of the theater group. Engaged in the indigenous movement, motivated at first by the participation of the older sister in the Organization of Indigenous Young Truká (OJIT), begins a fight during the occupation against the works and recovery of the Farm Antonio Lalinha, in Pernambuco banks of river, which encompassed the area of the construction site. Formed in Catholicism, he is also involved in social and youth movements of the Catholic Church. With intellectual, religious and political rhetoric calling, he weaves a discourse on the relationship between transposition of water and Truká cosmology: the existence of its people depends on the good condition of the river. To Maurílio, transposition become a river leg. He left the island on the side of Pernambuco, leaving them without the water. This would cause a great impact also in the Light Charms that inhabit the waters of the river. Perhaps the people would be forced to migrate, leaving the island, and would no longer be a tribe because they would lose the charms and are the charms is what makes them as such:

> [...] Turn this river leg we call small river, it would cease to be small river, because we would be without this water. Because this water would be exactly what would go on the channel. So for us this is a big impact when it comes to the Charms of Light. Because it is very easy we leave our people, somebody come and say. You will now have to get out of Assunção, they will have to go somewhere else . And what makes you stay in the fight, to believe in our own struggle, are the charms of Light and to know that if we get out of here, to know that people move, the people move, the Charm does not move. So people suffer for it. Can take, we can get out of here to somewhere else, but the Charm does not move, it remains in the

territory [...] So if we lose the water with the implementation, if we lose water, the water we call small river, we lose the Charm. He will procure, he will cease to exist. Because for us, for our people, the Charm is what is what we live for. So it can give good results. The waters. The Old Chico waters are enchanted to us, they have power. So, it is very easy there, I would not be Indian. What is the connection that I will have with the wisdom of my land, my people? What is the wisdom that I will have from my ancestors? (Maurilio).

The economy and the livelihood of the people living on the island absolutely depend on the waters of the river. There is no other source of water and all agriculture and livestock depends of rivers water through a pumping system. Planting of rice, onions, bananas, passion fruit, are all irrigated by the river. Goats, sheep, cattle, ducks, pigs and chickens depend on the same water as well as the people who live there, drink the water of the Old Chico.

Because we think on the zeal, the care, we think about surviving, and where we get our daily bread, is where our elders fish, where our parents seek to water our lands, and our plantations with it, with that beauty. Maybe people would leave it alone. (Maurilio).

In the narratives about the fate of Charms of Light, a logic emerges: there is a symbiosis between Truká Charms of Light and the river. The loss of water means the loss of charms and therefore the loss of themselves, their world, as it is known. And of course, in terms of material satisfaction, water is of utmost necessity for them. The rainfall is very low in the region with little precipitation of rain over the past few years. Without the river water, or even a decrease, the entire system of the island goes bankrupt.

Chief Neguinho, born in 1972, farmer, former councilor of Cabrobó, being well articulated in political leadership at national level, having gone to Congress several times representing indigenous peoples, worked throughout his life for indigenous rights, especially Truká since the youth forces began to fight to "retake" lands. He lived from small the island and remembers how the river was, ebb cultivation, the fish that lived in it and who were fishing for their livelihood and children's games on its banks:

Because here the river belongs to the natives, for you to get an idea, the boy's job at the time, my service of 10-year-old boy, was watering the ebb. It was the most tiring job than I've ever seen in my life. Parents of people were planting and gave a gourd for us to play with the water. Then you throw water and sank, threw water, play and sank. I had some ravines we had as a natural slide. I was playing with the bowl and slipped. So to scare us our parents said it was the otter who did it. They would say the otters would catch us. And I was scared to death of otters. The problem is that the otters were on the rocks, they climbed the schools of fish they were or on the rocks or in the cow waiting. They caught fish and went to over the rocks. The matriarch mainly. It came a bit when she beat her ass, just jumped and he caught it. We learned to fish with otters, because we'd had where the *línguas de vaca* (cow-tongues: Plant common on the region) with the canoe at the time of matrinchás (a type of fish), and let go of the paddle when she jumped, many fall into the canoe. We would singe the ember. And there was here also the black caiman and Bantam. The Bantam we did not see much than it was a large alligator that we called canoe alligator. So many species that we had in our youth, golden times [...] So, we tell the stories to our children of surubins parents of people who caught them. The surubins would be measured by feet. So these surubims were so big, had so many feet. 22, 23 feet. We didn't eat small fish. The size of a man, 2.30 meters, 2.4 meters surubim. Golden snapper as well. Golden snappers, they made up as well, that at the time that the water locked up in Sobradinho they had gone crazy, those made up this story about the fish being in the caneo's motor. You would see it and believe it, and it seemed like the way that would do things were never going to end. Then floods filled these two ponds, when the water lowered it was a source of wealth. When the time came for the river to go back to normal the fish also disappeared, then, where we had been fishing in the ponds. Then you were afraid to take from surubim season, or caboge season, or mandi, or other fishes that you do not see today. (Chief Neguinho).

When asked how the situation today is compared to the older times, he responds:

It is an ugly situation. People thought when I was a kid, we sometimes looked at the river there in Rio Grande, you looked at it and seemed that infinite thing, there is no greater river than this one, that it will never dry out. And when you arrive here by Sergipe, Alagoas there, it gives us such a great sorrow. [...] The Xocós of Alagoas, the guys caught a shark 3 km from the river channel. Because the water levesl lowered in the dams also, the lack of rain in this region, because the time has greatly helped this evaporation issue. The guys are catching a shark in the river bank. Then you are sure that the river is dying. Here, we had a temporary rivers for more than 15 years ago, when it rains also water runs. And it was raining and you got 6, 7, 8 months of water in a year. Sometimes we went with the canoes, as the people of the tribe we used the canoes often, to fish, fishing is decisive nowadays. There are no more auxiliary woods, all of it was destroyed. Okay, life expectancy of the river it is quite complicated and sometimes, we think it is not. This place where we live here. If the river didn't pass here, this would be uninhabited. (Chief Neguinho).

For Neguinho, the struggle for the Truká and their rights, including the use of water, doesn›t dissociate of its precepts and religious rituals. In them, the people Truká work with the Charms, entities that inhabit the waters and forests, in a reciprocal relationship in which humans, non-human and nature are in symbiosis:

The culture of Truká the toré of our people is a toré a lot of strength. Because our toré is also provided [...] I do not know if you will get the chance to see or will have the opportunity to see a toré our toré is given to the strength of the people showing what are the elements of nature. Our songs are for both the water and to the woods.
[…]
We dance it when we are sad, when have a great loss, on times of "retaking" or when we have re-vindicated ourselves. Already the Mesa and in Particular, it is more focused towards our ancestors, our Charms, it is a time to take advice, to ask for strength, to add strength. I would say it is the most sacred time for us. And toré is our daily life, the trajectory of the history of our people looks like a big toré
[…]
Does the simple Indian who lives there in the fields have the same understanding as us? - He does! When we say that he will lose

something, that will be impacted by this and that, he leaves and heads to the rock in the fields and dance the torezinho with us and come to ask for strength to God and the Charms of light to overcome any given obstacles. So I hope you not only talk with the staff for the ritual, you will be surprised by a lot in a lot of things they put into them, more than you will have the opportunity to meet. (Chief Neguinho).

The conversations and interviews in the village of Cajueiro, the interlocutors talked about the environmental impact of the Sobradinho dam and the deterioration of the river. One of the impacts of the dam, perceived by them, quite emphatically, was the reduction of the water volume, eliminating the natural movement of flood and ebb it had before. It was this movement of the river that allowed the people that lived close by to cultivate in low tide, taking advantage of the flow of water to plant on more fertile soil. With the impossibility of this planting technique, everyone on the island had to resort to irrigation by pumping. On the other hand, the fact that the water no longer "washes the river" with regular floods, causes an accumulation of plants on the banks that causes an unbalance on the river system and promote silting. Another important perceived impact was the decrease in fish, which, in many cases, without the occurrence of spawning, died out, the rise of the tide for fish breeding was prevented by the dam. Chief Dão says:

It hurt us here. In the place where we would shower once, I and others, nowadays is Land. It has no more ebbing, when I met the river I met it with an ebb. The river was filled all year and leaked, it cleansed itself every year and there was no need to sweep it, then came the water up, and when it came down it cleaned everything. Today, the Sobradinho dam, which never brought profit to us, reduced the waters tide, the river does not fill more like it used to, right. It no longer cleanses the islands, I no longer have that business: I will just plant ebb. I'll tell you nowadays, I used to plant ebb, my father and my mother, who taught me, we used to plant ebb. But what if you plant today ebb you die of hunger, there is no more ebbing.
[...]

> A month or two went by, watering the soil when the tide lowered then you planted potatoes, cassava, pluck beans, string beans, corn.
> [...]
> The river is getting far away from where it used to be, away from where we knew the river, where it was, because it no longer does more cleaning and the weeds are taking over. The fish we had on the river: mandi, massarapó, matrinchã, golden, catfish, are [in] facing extinction. Catfish, golden, Mandin, one blue, pirá. Do you still see an pacuzinho, curimatá a Canana a cari a arezinho a xotó, which are fish that we have the most. (Chief Dão).

These changes in the environment are accompanied by cultural changes, habits and customs, relations between young and old, men and women, old and new, traditional and modern are being confronted and negotiated, transforming culture, stimulating values, *ethos* and worldviews. Nature and culture don't oppose here, they interconnect, to interfere and change. Economy and religion are not formed as separate and different structures, they intersect and influence each other:

> Because our tradition here during Easter Week, it is the month that you eat fish [...] Older people do not even eat meat any way. It's just the same fish [...] My grandmother, my mother. I cannot bear to do it, I go and have some meat. Now, there only one day that I do not eat meat, which is Friday. Because my grandmother said: "Damn it, do not eat at least on Friday." Then, on Friday, I do not eat meat. Things are changing and the people are also changing, becoming modern. (Chief Dão).

For Bertinho, the Chief who succeeded Dão in 2015, the main concern is a cultural change that disrupts the traditional ancestral worship of Charms of Light. Bertinho is also a religious leader, shaman in the initiation phase, but already commands rituals of Toré, Mesa and others. He is sought for treatments, healing the sick and initiating boys in religion. His abilities for spiritual work and his knowledge make him a religious leader that attracts many people from the village to the rituals. As a young man was also one of the founders of the Organization of Indigenous Young Truká (OJIT) in 1999. He says:

What draws more attention to me, these days is modified things, other religions are entering and our people leaving worship nature behind, they are leaving behind the value the thing of the earth, the things that we were created from.

[...]

Arriving at the foot tree of a Jurema (spiritual ritual) and to have humility to ask that tree to extract that plant, for us to make a remedy for a person, nowadays, we are losing that. We get in the river and we ask permission to our Mother of Water, which is the Charm of water for us to enter into the river for us to fish, and those are the things that are fading slowly. (Bertinho).

The threatened cosmology and apocalyptic eschatology Truká

During the research, everyday festivities and ritual were observed, through participation and dialogue, always listening to their stories, covering several villages of the island and also talking to leaders and elders of the villages. In our conversations with young people and adults, one sees an effort, in their speeches and narratives, in stating two fundamental precepts for them: the political struggle within the indigenous movement and related social movements and a religion based on two rituals, the Toré and Mesa. Both have the memory Acilon Ciriaco as the most important reference regarding the struggle for lands, inspired by the Charms, especially by Captain Bernardino.

Traditional Truká religion is quite complex, dynamic and diverse. They are devotees of various entities, between Catholic saints and nature›s beings, they celebrate parties and also practice rituals such as Our Lady of the Assunção Feast, the St. Goncalo feast, Penance, Easter Week, Cosme and Damian Party and, Toré and Mesa. Lately, some Indians have converted to a new Pentecostal church, which is not very well accepted on the island. The coexistence between different religious traditions, conflicts and confluences form a mosaic too complex. The inter-influence of Catholicism and the cult of the Holy Jurema, practiced both in

Toré as Mesa seems to be more structured and widespread event throughout the island, being experienced differently among different groups. In Cajueiro village, I was accompanied, more closely, by a group of related and neighboring people, working spiritually with enough force and regularity. This group has provided some clues for understanding the Truká spirituality, especially to understand their cosmology.

The cult of Jurema presents a broad and diverse tradition in the Brazilian Northeast and, these days, is expanding to other parts of the country. Each indigenous village from the North-East and every yard of tradition can tell the origin of their beliefs and rank a pantheon of different entities, according to their own historical and spiritual processes. According to the Truká, God would have passed for an old caboclo, an Old man, the ancestor of Truká, the wisdom of the Holy Jurema, Scientific Jurema. Such knowledge would be basically in the preparation of wine, from the bark of black *jurema thornless*, the anjucá, and how to teach it within both rituals, either the Toré, or Mesa. Although confluent, both rituals are placed by the Indians themselves as different, especially because the Toré is done publicly and has an identity connotation and more vehement policy. The Toré wheels were held in protest against the PEC 215[83] during the occupation of roads BR 116 and BR 316, in 2014, which brought together five ethnic groups of Pernambuco Hinterlands. The Mesa, also known as the Particular ritual (Batista, 2005), on the contrary, it is a closed ritual, with few people, usually held at someone's house requested for specific reason, such as an illness or evil spirit, or own traditional officiating.

Both rituals evoke Catholic entities as Our Lady of the Assunção, São Francisco, caboclas entities and, Charms of Light. The Charms have a strong correspondence with the elements of nature, many of them lived on earth as Indians in the past, and are ancestors of the Truká currently. Among them there are: Mother of ‹Water, who lives in the depths of the São Francisco River, in the spiritual city full of gold; Captain Bernardino and Captain John Duardo, which are juremeiros teachers, ancestors and founders of the village that sometimes are present in the closed rituals. Besides them, several entities as Mariner, Master Zé Pilintra are rituals.

---

83 The Proposed Constitutional Amendment 215 is one that, if approved

For each Master or Charm chants are presented to each that are also called lines, which function is to invoke the forces that are present in the Mesa and Toré. In their holdings, they often advise and promote healing of certain ailments, and the affliction rituals as fundamental to aid conflict resolution and disease. Working with Charms of Light was essential to Acilon Ciriaco and his friends «to upraise the village» and, even today, are important for their support. For continuity, the spirits themselves summon people to become their spokesmen and perform the spiritual works.

In conversation with Dão and Bertinho, they were asked: "With the transposition of the São Francisco River, where to the Charms live? What about Mother of Water and other Charms that live in the water, how do they live? " Both replied:

> Chief Dão: they live in sadness.
>
> Chief Bertinho: everyone is saddened by the loss of water, right. They are saddened by the devastation that the people are doing with pollutants being released into the river, the waters, they are sad, they are angry and nature itself revolts against humanity, many disasters, many waters of the sea are rising and ravaging the cities, it is the water Charm himself, the force of nature even if it is bringing change for the men who are doing it with the water, with nature, deforesting all. Playing the city of garbage, sewage, all in the water, he is killing his own life, because without water the human being cannot survive. Years from now, when searching for a safe drinking water, the water will be all polluted. That is when they will open their eyes, but it will be too late already.

With all the work and projects that have impacted along the river have caused to populations and Caatinga of Pernambuco hinterlands, perhaps it is already too late. Too late for the Court of Audits (TCU) to charge revitalization actions from the Brazilian government, hitherto considered unsatisfactory. Too late for ANA disclose the basin of São Francisco is committed to its hydrologist condition and that it is damaging the reservoirs. [84] It is too late, for it experiences the feeling that climate change, excessive tragedies and lack of water undertake life throughout the country.

The relationship between modern societies based on industrial production, consumption, market, and nature; the environment, has been exploited and devastated. The various actors involved in high-impact projects such as construction of power plants, large agricultural enterprises, mining, etc., think, plan and negotiate gains, benefits or mitigations of well-differentiated forms. Traditional villages involved, such as indigenous, quilombolas , tide-and fishermen, have questioned

---

84 Court of Audit (2015), 'TCU oversees recovery actions Revitalization Program Basin São Francisco River', accessed 28 may 2016 at http://portal.tcu.gov.br/imprensa/noticias/tcu -fiscaliza-shares-of-the-recovery-program-of-revitalization-of-basin-Hydrographic-the-river-are-francisco.htm .

and opposed to these works strongly since they have shocked their daily lives, ruled in family relationships and subsistence economic activities and less impact. It is possible to see a variety of positions, perspectives and concepts, as well as ways of negotiating. Among the various interpretations regarding the various impacts of large projects by the government and private companies, it is clear, in focus, with the Truká that motivated by traditional cosmology. How do they think about ecology, the relationship between humans and nature, from the point of view of their religious beliefs? How do non-human beings think who live in nature or are the very nature? This is not only to understand how the Amerindians think of the destruction of forests, rivers, scrublands, savannas, but think of the relationship between man and the environment from its own perspective. This is not to perform an interpretive activity of the ideas from local cosmologies, however, a dialogue, taking seriously the belief expressed in such cosmologies as the possibility of perspective transformation, habits and action in the world.

For Bertinho, the Charms of water, beings of power that inhabit the waters of the São Francisco River, are saddened by the pollution of rivers, with impacts that have been suffering for decades. They say that if the water leave with the transposition, the Charms of water will also leave as well. If they are, what will become of the Truká living under his protection? What will become of the Truká, Riverines, tide-fishermen, Quilombolas, farmers, entire populations that inhabit the towns along the São Francisco River and have no other source of water to survive with?

The perception of the São Francisco River integration project, from Truká cosmology, allows us to observe, in reverse, the different interpretations of the process of death of river experts, scientists and technicians. The issue of drought during spring and the Sobradinho dam is not being affected by the river transposition project, since they were not yet linked to the bombs that will make the flow of water. Although it seems obvious, from the perspective of technical knowledge from the perspective of learning from magic, traditional, of Truká, the dissatisfaction of the water beings, the Charms of Light, could cause ecological disasters in different places, because to respond to the holistic logic, according to which everything is interconnected in a cycle of influences that are related. Thus, the end of the water is the end of the Charms, it is nature giving the change across the country. If the Charms of Light appear in Bertinho speech as synonyms of nature, or forces of nature, the Charms of water appear as a being who commands strength wisely and is the energy of the water, it is the nature of a living being that suffers with human actions and react to these actions causing an imbalance that will threaten the life of the human beings on the planet. In this case, the logic of Truká cosmology, the force of the water is not running only downstream, but also upstream. When you open a channel to bring the waters of the river, it will affect other waters elsewhere, or if your vision is holistic and helps to better understand the source that drought is a result of devastation elsewhere beyond. We must see that the problem is planetary and that the works of the water transfer project cannot be causing, directly, the dry spring, but they also contribute, together with other projects, to the death of the São Francisco River.

Not be able perceive or hide the future impact the flow of 2% of the river water in this process of destruction, promoted by the Brazilian government, contrary to the holistic perspective of Bertinho and Truká cosmology. A project is ongoing and is not to revitalize the river but create a serious struggle for what remains of it, in a few years. One thing is connected to another and this is what you should learn the Amerindian cosmology.

The river›s death predictions and large migratory processes arising lead to think about the eschatological predictions Bertinho, in his reasoning, changing the course of the river as it is being done is not an action that moves only with a river arm, it is to put in course much larger forces than the white man can imagine. The results are more complex and potentially of catastrophic dimensions indeed. The impact of the project is already large in itself, without assessing what will happen to the river when its waters travel the canal. It will impact on public finances, on regional populations, on the daily lives of people, culture, religion, family relations, the regional economy. The result? Still far from seeing some results in objective terms, which is to bring water to the population of Paraiba and Ceara Hinterlands. Perhaps it will not even arrive. Place your bets.

Pipipá: A little of its history

The Pipipá are inserted in the context of "resurgent people", as well as Truká within actions that reintegrates through an identity and recognition process, ethno-genesis, i.e. "historical process of emergence of a socially effective border collectivities, distinguishing them and organizing the interaction between social subjects who recognize themselves and are recognized as belonging to them "(Barreto Filho, 1999, p.93 cited Barbosa, 2001).One of the most significant elements for the ethnic affirmation is the historical rescue, symbologies and rituals as cultural heritage.

The resurgence of Pipipá (Barbosa, 2001) is included in the crisis that began in May 1998, within the Kambiwá indigenous area, when they considered the deposition of Pajé Expedito Roseno. The onset crisis resulted in the election of leaders of Chief and Pajé. The "schism" among the group came from a standstill in the election results, generating the output Expedito Roseno and ethno-genesis Pipipá. Leading a group of six families, the Pajé moved to the *Travessão do Ouro* village, located within the boundaries of the indigenous area demarcated Kambiwá. From there, they went on to lead five other villages. The break between the people was expressed symbolically by burning the "maracas", "cataiobas" instruments and ritual garments used in the Toré dance. The split will be represented in the design of rituals: the Toré dance as opposed to the dance of the "beach", which is characteristic of Kambiwá and binds them to Pankararu.

Pipipá is a tribe who resisted colonization through alliances with other peoples of semi-arid Pernambuco, with a history akin to the Truká, the division of land grants, the incursion of Europe in promoting a project «civilizing". There are records from the eighteenth century, which refer to an attack order issued by Governor Luiz Lobo da Silva against the Indians who inhabited the Serra Negra:

> About the assault that the angry Gentile Pipipans and Paraquiós made in Moxotó the river, on August 28, 1759, and which resulted in some deaths (Archangel, 2003, p. 46).

The Pipipá and Xocó, at that time were already identified this way, continued to be pursued and it were spreading through the savanna and taking refuge in the highest mountains. Around 1802, settlements were installed by the Capuchin friars who rallied these groups near Serra Negra. Over the years, their lands were disputed by squatters and eventually were dispersed and mix with other indigenous groups in order to survive. Currently, the group rearticulated by separating from another nation, the Kambiwá, in whose land they lived and await the legal process of land ownership by the FUNAI.

In addition to waiting for the legalization of land tenure, which certainly leaves them vulnerable, another problem of legitimacy about these people: there are controversies regarding Pipipá name. Give meaning to the name is one of the Pajé search scopes, a process is underway and is part of the oral tradition. Expedito Roseno says it refers to the traditional indigenous name of the mountain, a clear ancestral identification with reinforcement of territorial space, in Particular the Serra Negra, its considered sacred land.

As noted Archangel (2003), the "inter-ethnic situations" originated from this tribe. In the past, they coalesced to resist, apparently while diluting Pipipá without, however, are no longer Indians. Now they spread to resurface, performing new joints to emerge as Pipipá, identity coined within a network of cultural exchange in the territory domain of different ethnicities.

The Serra Negra in Pipipá cosmology

Biological Reserve of Serra Negra (REBIO Serra Negra) was established by Decree No. 87591 of September 20, 1982 .It has an area of 1,044 hectares, the largest part inserted in the Caatinga biome there are altitude Swamp formations. His relationship with Pipipá is of great importance, including spiritual, considered vital in the cosmology of this tribe.

The Pipipá are often cited in the document of centuries of Brazilian colonization (XV-XIX centuries), known as inhabitants of the Serra Negra. But that did not favor the dispute for the territory.

In 1824, even before the Land Law (1850), for an inventory document property, the «heirs» of the land on which is the Serra Negra, acquired a century earlier, took the Indians their right to the land and its fields. The unwritten population had to undergo quite strange notarial bureaucracy to their cultural universe. Then came the idea to mix with other tribes to strengthen the resistance. But their struggle against the documentation was interpreted generally as illegitimate, not only by the existence of heritage documents and possession, as well as suggested tackling the idea of "progress" disseminated at the time.

The Republic of Brazil, and its governmental decisions on the Serra Negra were still without resolving deadlocks. Getulio Vargas created in 1934, the first Brazilian Forest Code [85], which advocated against the economic profit of existing elements in the forests. As an institution in charge of protecting natural resources, was founded in 1967, the Brazilian Institute for Forestry Development (IBDF), a federal agency under the Ministry of Agriculture. According to Nivaldo Neto[86], in memory of indigenous interlocutors, they did not take into account the Serra Negra. This was a period of proliferation of Conservation Units (UCs), created and managed without the consultation of affected populations.

With the dismantling of IBDF in 1989, IBAMA through its agents and subsequently surfaces in 2007, the creation of the Chico Mendes Institute for Biodiversity Conservation (ICMBIO), responsible for the management of protected areas. For the Indians, the ICMBIO engages in discriminatory actions, which leads to revolts by them, as occurred in the 'Indigenous April' in the year 2013, on the campus of the Federal University of Pernambuco (UFPE), in Recife.

The greatest support for these claims is the group's legitimacy itself, recognized by the state, their identity as indigenous people. In it, it is part of the notion of "territorial", redefining the social control over natural resources. The core is the legitimacy of access to ancestral

---

85 Decree No. 186. Accessed may 13th 2016 at http://www.planalto.gov.br/ ccivil_03/decreto/1930-1949/d23793.htm .

86 Neto, Nivaldo Aureliano Leo (2015), "'Nós somos os donos': conflitos socioambientais entre os índios Pipipã de Kambixuru e o ICMBIO no sertão de Pernambuco", accessed may 20th 2016 at http://eventos.livera.com.br /trabalho/98-1020291_25_06_2015_10-44-30_9459.PDF.

land and spiritual relationships of the indigenous group, today prevented by environmental legislation.

In Pipipá cosmology, they need the Serra Negra for the ritual known as Auricuri, which takes place annually from 10 to 20 October and in which only Indians can participate, except those authorized sporadically, which can follow for a few moments. In this period, toré rituals are daily, and take place every night. There, according to Nivaldo Neto, who was allowed to participate, an intense transaction of knowledge that reinforces old ties of reciprocity and establish many others. During the time the Auricuri, make contact with their former, present loved ones or that have become Charms of Light. These are times of spiritual empowerment, identity and learning. These ten days of October that Pipipá remain in Serra Negra are considered as lessons, bringing together male and female teachers, students and experts in certain knowledge. Classes are held in the woods amid makeshift huts, constituting phenomena of experience from certain environmental conditions. The importance of the Serra Negra to the Indians, Pipipá and Kambiwá, is the ritual that refers to specific forms of territorial logic.

The eastern axis of transposition on Pipipá lands

The Pipipá have five villages. Four are located in the territory staked by the Kambiwá tribe, who temporarily ceded part of its territory to the Pipipá. The fifth village is in the only Pipipá recognized territory.

The *Travessão do Ouro* village, near the Serra do Periquito, is the administrative epicenter of this tribe, where the Chief lives, the Shaman and a majority Pipipá; the Serra Negra village, the eponymous mountain range has a great religious and ritualistic meaning which is nearby, is in the vacating process, except possibly when the space is for Aricuri rituals; Capoeira do Barro is the village where the non-Indians are settled, through an initiative of the INCRA to profile settlements, however, was recently occupied by Pipipá who perform toré in that site; Faveleira village is hybridized with Indians and non-Indians there is also a functioning school and health clinic. Caraíbas is a village located near the Serra do Talhado and Serrote Tamanduá, made of small landowners who, not taking other ethnonym, identify themselves as Pipipá.

In the fifth village Pipipá, Caraíbas some water reservoirs were installed that are supplied periodically by trucks, with just enough water for human consumption. The east axis of the channels transposition goes through significant part of its territory. It is possible to observe how devastating was the work for the site. In addition to the channel itself, there will be a reservoir or huge dam, and for its construction, a large area was completely cleared. Mister Benedito, also known as Caboclo, is one of the leaders of the village, talks about the devastation in the village:

> [...] Worse than when they did this one channel, no one talked about the deforestation that was going to happen ... because we did not think it would be a huge deforestation of such size, right? [...] The place were people take food for the animals ... why here a time of Hinterland of that here ... in the dry season, the goat has to take macambira, mandacaru for the animals, for creation, for everything, and where he spent channel ended all [...] that there was a great loss because they killed a lot of trees that served as medicine ... is ... these trees that they cleared serve to remedy [...] is the imburana, mastic is the Quixabeira, is the tariff iron, this is all stick medicine, serves remedy, and they ended up with all the same ... (Caboclo).

Despite the injury caused, there is between them some expectation that the water in the reservoir is available through a capture tap:

> [...] But I believe they had the right to explain how this dam was going to get done, no one knows when they fill this dam will be with water to benefit the animals ... or not ... [...] the staff are very suspicious that idea of "ah, maybe they will get water for us," perhaps not ... [...] I cannot explain how it the water will come all the way from the dam ... because if they wanted to help the people here, they could have built closer to us. From this point, you are 3 km away, 3 km is far. If they wanted do something for the people here ... (Caboclo).

There would have been, by the technicians, a vague promise of access to water, «a tap» for the Pipipá. However, there are dark suspicions. One is that both the reservoir / dam as channel would be fenced and made inaccessible. The Chief Valdemir says this was already happening in the other two reservoirs east axis, near the Floresta municipality. Benedito said, "or they will surround everything ... there on the edge of this channel is already the position in several places, it is ready now ... they will surround this channel." That is, poles for fencing were being placed. The Truká said something similar in relation to the channel next to them.

Besides water, the Pipipá, demanded, the technicians responsible for the work, to build catwalks over the channel, for humans and animals, despite promises, they have not yet been built.

Another question that looms is that, as the territory is not marked, if there is demarcation, there is fear that the government excludes the area through which the channel is being built and the reservoir. If this happens, it will be a huge loss territorial loss for the Pipipá tribe.

Distrust, Caboclo reveals, in relation to what is being done is great:

> [...]There is certitude they are benefiting from this... making dams to benefit from them, the channel, because when filling these dams ... one carries water through the channel and is water there from the São Francisco River ... another dam, the first dam which they did, which was the first they got ready, that one overflows with water... the water, it's almost like a river right ... she's already carrying water to other dam right in the middle [...] now I believe this water will greatly benefit are those who are wealthy, these rich people ... maybe she'll do much benefit to breeding to fish and those things, right? (Caboclo).

Chapter III: The Struggles

Completed surveys in the vicinity, and collected weapons and ammunition of war, the gunmen gathered the corpses that lay scattered at various points. They beheaded us. They burned the bodies. Then lined up the heads on two roadsides, regularly spaced, is fronting-, oped faces to the path. Above, the highest marginal bushes, they suspended the remaining uniforms, pants and multi-colored dolmans (military helmet), saddles, belts, caps of crimson stripes, coats, blankets, water bottles and backpacks ...

The withered and bare Caatinga appeared suddenly blossoming in extravagant red color on the currents, the faint blue of dolmans and living glares of the plates of the oscillating Talins and stirrups ... (Cunha, 1984, p.156)[87]

The third part of *Os Sertões* (The Hinterlands) called *The Struggles*, chronicles of the four Brazilian Army expeditions sent to suppress the Canudos rebellion, which brought approximately twenty thousand people together. It approaches also, in a meticulous way, the battles between the two groups, at which Euclides da Cunha surprises and elevates the strength and bravery of the Hinterland men in coping against the republican troops, which is to say that Canudos did not surrender, despite the defeat.

According Walnice Galvão (2009), this war is not limited, nor is it explained as a mere revolt against the Republic, which was suggested by the press at the time, it was inspired by the conservative peasant revolt. According to Galvao, the Canudos express it as the revolt of poor people who have absolutely nothing, who have become followers of leader Antonio Conselheiro, abandoning their world and creating new forms of sociability. With this "it engendered an alternative power structure that subtracted the behest of farmers, priests and police chiefs - who embodied the highest authorities in the Hinterlands, representing private property, the church and the forces of repression" (Galvão, 2009)[88] .

---

87   Cunha, Euclides (1984), *Os Sertões*, São Paulo: Três, Biblioteca do Estudante.
88   Introduction 3rd edition of Os Sertões.

Today, acts of resistance involving struggles against the implementation of development projects that dismantle the traditional ways of life and destroy the environment does not involve Canudos. There are no images of bloodshed in the bushes, there is resistance, there is the army and other elements composing the scene, but there is no actual war. Still, as the insurgents of Canudos, opponents, those who refuse the supposedly works of "modernization" that compromise their traditional lifestyle, usually take the same taint of being backward and against "progress." It creates barriers for development projects.

Speaking at the opening of a biodiesel plant in Mato Grosso, in November 2006, Lula highlights the need for growth and development for the country, for him, it was necessary to take down the "the barriers that I have with the environment, all obstacles with the prosecution, all obstacles with the quilombolas issue, the issue of Brazilian Indians, all the obstacles that we have in the Audit of Court (TCU) [...][89]. This is a statement[90], possibly improvised, which expresses exactly how the government implemented projects like Belo Monte and the transposition of the São Francisco River facing resistance to his model of modernization and development of the country.

In the case of the São Francisco River the transposition project, there were many legal struggles, political - among them indigenous - against the development. They were systematic, relentless, but, like the "modernization process" of Brazil, in progress at the time of Euclides da Cunha wrote the Hinterlands, it was managed in a exclusive mode. In a shady game of make-believe, the Government summoned the parties to be heard when, in practice, carried speech that progress and modernization are the means to save everyone through great development projects. Added to this the number of superficial revitalization projects and the incongruity with the actual conditions

---

89 Carta Maior (2006), 'Entidades repudiam declaração de Lula sobre povos tradicionais', accessed on February 20th 2016 at http://www.cartamaior.com.br/?/Editoria/Meio-Ambiente/Entidades-repudiam-declaracao-de-Lula-sobre-povos-tradicionais/3/12236.

90 This unfortunate statement was repudiated in a document signed by ABONG, Brazilian Center for Cultural Reference Foundation (Cebrac), the Amazon Working Group (GTA), the Ethos Institute for Social Responsibility, the Socio-Environmental Institute (ISA) and the Coordination of Indigenous Organizations Brazilian Amazon (Coiab).

of the river, were planned even before the official inauguration of the project and they did not show viability.

Fighting with laws and courts

Article 225 of the 1988 Constitution states that "everyone has the right to an ecologically balanced environment, of common use and essential to a healthy quality of life, imposing to the government and society the duty to defend it and preserve it for present and future generations." What is noticeable, however, is that there is a real danger of environmental damage with the project, or the project violating the Constitution.

The Law 9.433/97, which the Federal Government had finally created the National System of Water Resources, already regulates item XIX of Art. 21 of the Constitution. This law establishes the shared management of water resources and created the Basin Committees. The Committee of the Hydrographic Basin of the São Francisco River (CBHSF) approved the withdrawal of water from the East Axis, provided exclusively and demonstrably intended for human and animal consumption, but which was solemnly disregarded.

In a situation of water scarcity, on an emergency basis, in accordance with the law, the appeal should be used primarily for human consumption and watering livestock. The government itself assumes that water is a scarce resource in the region, but even so, according to the Ministry of Integration, 70% of the incorporated water would be for irrigation, 26% for urban and industrial use and only 4% for human consumption population of Caatingas. And it is around this last point, negligible compared to the others, that the government justifies the project. These inconsistencies with the law generated a series of clashes in the legal sphere. Actions, opinions and recommendations were processed by the courts of Brazil. Still, the federal government ignored it and began the work on the transposition.

The Order of Lawyers of Brazil - Sectional Sergipe (OAB/SE) - in April 2007, actively participated in this clash, which left the most serious complaints. By the Central Union of Workers of the State of Sergipe and the Social Pastoral of the Roman Catholic Archdiocese of Aracaju, implemented a Civil Action Originating (ACO 1003) against the transposition project in the Supreme Court. In the lawsuit, the Brazilian Bar Association requested that the Union, Ibama and the National Water Agency (ANA) immediately paralyzed the implementation of the project.

Several irregularities were scored, such as the violation of the powers of the Basin Committee of the São Francisco River and the Master Plan for Water Resources, the lack of evidence in the Union's argument, and no oversight of the limits of the rights the consumer is granted, fails the Environmental Impact Assessment (EIA) and Environmental Impact Report (RIMA), the total lack of sustainability of the project and the absence of federal pact for implementation.

The legal battles were controversial. According to Minister Sepúlveda Pertence, in the injunction (ACO 876, 2006, p.14-16), handed down on December 18, 2006, which in summary, the arguments used in pending lawsuits and petitions by the Supreme Court sought to stop the environmental licensing and revoke the preliminary environmental license 2000/2005 and, ultimately, prevent the implementation of the Transposition Project.

The listed reasons were many. Errors and omissions in the relevant EIA/RIMA, especially to ignore the environmental, social and economic impact in the mining by the bay and part of the basin; there is no consideration of technological alternatives and the project location, as prescribed in art.5 °, of Res. CONAMA n.01/86; the disregard of the Upper and Middle Region São Francisco, the areas in directly affected by the project; technical inaccuracies water resources of the basin, hydroelectric and proposed hydro sanitary systems; failure to comply with the monitoring requirements of the certificate of municipalities affected by the project; the absence of congressional authorization for the realization of the project, as there are uses of water resources in indigenous lands, according to art. 231, §3, the CF/88; the fact that the Ten-Year Plan of the Basin (2004-2013) have been ignored; the National Water Resources Policy disrespected; the impracticability of conducting the public hearings before the short time lapse between the date of designation and its effective implementation and considerable distance from the places where they would carry out the audience of the people directly concerned; vices in the adoption of Resolution no.411 issued by ANA in the absence of the manifestation of the Technical Board; granting the preliminary license 200/2005, despite failures and omissions made by the EIA/RIMA and without being nurtured effective popular participation.

According to the minister, the opposing party (IBAMA, Ministry of National Integration and the Union) countered, the preliminary decision, claiming compliance with the legal requirements; the holding of public hearings and the granting of the preliminary environmental license does not mean the completion of licensing or even the start of work and therefore new and further clarifications and additions where necessary the EIA/RIMA could arise from inquiries taken at hearings; that the granting of the preliminary license does not cause any harm to the environment, because they had not initiated the physical works of the project; with regard to the irregularities in tenders and contracts relating to works, it was added to put forward the Union that the Ministry of National Integration has only issued the first notice in order to hire a specialized company to provide technical support to the Ministry of Integration in order to obtain the environmental permits; active illegitimacy of some of the authors entities.

Finally, the Minister Sepúlveda Pertence ordered on December 18, 2006 for all injunctions to suspend the environmental licensing process. In the next section, we discuss the circumstances and the context that provided this cancellation.

From this decision, the Ministry of National Integration continued the licensing application and once the previous was rectified, the license was granted. The installation license was granted on March 23, 2007 (ACO 876, 2006, p.46-50).

The Federal Regional Court of the 1st Region accepted the request of the Federal Public Ministry and suspended it again, the PISF projects in December 2007. For the MPF, the project could not have been approved by the National Water Resources Council (CNRH) for three reasons: the water supply pleaded for implementation in the subject of an administrative procedure in the Basin Committee of the São Francisco River, which still had not been analyzed; the project violated the Water Resources Plan for targeting the economic use of water use; the project also violates the principles of decentralized water management and popular participation established by the National Water Resources Policy (Law n. 9.433/97).

In the same month, the Supreme Court overturned the injunction granted by the Federal Court and dismissed the grievance filed by the Attorney General of the Republic, also denying the provision of regimental grievances filed by the parties "without a legitimate" process, respecting the request of the Attorney General's Office.

In regards to ANA, the grant award, not only failed to consider relevant technical aspects but also invalidated the decisions of the Committee, it failed to meet issues related to the basin's management, for example, conflicts and distribution of the social burdens. To be limited to the statement that there was a water availability to carry out the project, aggravated more the conflicts in the region, mainly between recipients and donor states, jeopardizing present and future uses. also prevented relevant advisory uses for the region, in particular the generation of electricity and the maintenance of the river and coastal ecosystem associated with the mouth of the river.

Amid these disputes and their time-consuming decisions, continuing to release in May 2007, four battalions of the 1st Combat Engineer Regiment, based in João Pessoa (PB), installed their sites in the municipalities of Cabrobó and Floresta (PE). The projects under military supervision would be the construction of channels connecting the São Francisco River to the pumping stations of the water, the two axes of transposition, and the opening roads connecting major highways to pumping stations. At this point, the construction of stations, decided through bidding, was borne by the private sector. All contractors (Odebrecht, Andrade Gutierrez, Queiroz Galvão, Mendes Junior, Camargo Corrêa, Schahin and OAS) that made offers which were later denounced for corruption in Operation Car Wash[91]. The army did not escape fraud allegations either[92] in the projects they

---

91 G1 Globo.com (2015),), '7 das 10 maiores empreiteiras tiveram executivos investigados na lava-jato', accessed 10 september 2016 at http://g1.globo.com/politica/operacao-lava-jato/noticia/2015/06/7-das-10-maiores-empreiteiras-tiveram-executivos-investigados-na-lava-jato.html.

92 Direito do Estado (2011), 'Investigações apuram envolvimento de militares em fraudes nas obras do PAC', accessed 10 september 2016 at http://www.direitodoestado.com.br/noticias/investigacoes-apuram-envolvimento-de-militares-em-fraudes-nas-obras-do-pac.

participated, and the authenticity of these complaints remains yet, to date, to be proven.

At the same time the legal battle goes to court, the cornerstone of the project was launched back in 2007, by the Minister[93] Geddel Vieira Lima, who took the opportunity to hold a meeting with community leaders, religious and political figures and rebutted criticism of transposition projects.

The Political Struggle: the hunger strike at Caravana

One of the most significant oppositions to how the transposition project was made comes from the Brazilian Semi-Arid Articulation (ASA). The association defends expectations of benefits that the project has not outweigh the losses related to riparian forests of the region and the marine fauna and especially the neglect of traditional groups, in addition to the compulsory output riparian owners, with the loss of surrounding lands to the channels. According to the manifesto signed by the organization, "the São Francisco transposition passes over indigenous communities, traditional agriculture, favors largely the major producers and, instead of democratizing water, they accumulate it"[94]

As a viable alternative, the ASA supports the effectiveness of the One Million Cisterns program, which also started during the period of the first government of former President Luiz Inacio Lula da Silva in 2003.

A Complaint Report was formulated[95], with the participation of nine indigenous peoples in their workmanship, on the impacts that

---

93 Bahia Notícias (2007), 'Rio São Francisco: maratona pelo nordeste' accessed April 12th 2016 at http://www.bahianoticias.com.br/noticia/2159-rio-sao-francisco-maratona-pelo nordeste.html>.

94 ASA Brasil (2009), 'ASA na mídia', accessed January 4th 2015 at http: <//www. asabrasil.org.br/imprensa/asa-na-midia?artigo_id=9391.

95 CIMI complaint Report (2007), 'Povos indígenas impactados com a transposição do rio São Francisco', accessed September 15th 2015 at http://www.cimi. org.br/pub/publicacoes/1241549933_relatapoinmetransp.pdf.

the projects had on them. According to the document, a study sponsored by the World Bank, which made a very thorough analysis of
irrigation in the semiarid region, with a view to study the correlation
between irrigated agriculture and poverty alleviation in the region,
says that during the last three decades, we invested over $2 billion of
public funds in projects related to irrigation, for the supply of 200,000
hectares in the semiarid region, of which 140,000 were considered
productive. All of these features, according to the report were leaked
by the aforementioned drought industry, which extended throughout
Brazil and is feared for its continuity.

In 2005, the transposition project began to take shape and, as
it approached its execution and the controversy regarding it escalated,
involving legal action and civil protests. One of the first demonstrations came from CBHSF[96], which demanded a full suspension of any
initiative linked to the transposition project until a "Basin Plan" was
drafted, the National Water Agency (ANA) canceled all suspended
activities. Meaning that, if the Committee itself recognized legal
forum debates and deliberations regarding the basin of São Francisco
had issues against the transposition it implies that the government,
was in a rush. If it was such an important issue for the region, a lot of
study and dialogue was needed to establish a project of this magni-
tude. It is also necessary to point out that the Committee is not part
of the Government, but the ANA is, and to bypass their own technical agency to not only disallow important sectors but also suggest that
there were other interests agreed upon the project.

The Ten-Year Plan CBHSF prescribes as priority uses: a) internal use (within the basin), in cases of shortage for human consumption and watering livestock; b) use for restricted and exclusive productive input for internal uses of the basin. In addition to establishing the
priority uses and other elements of the water management of the São
Francisco River Basin, "the Ten-Year Plan provides that only 360m³/s
can be allocated (awarded), of which 335 have already been. Over
then 25 m³/s are left for current and future use of multiple uses, with

---

96 Authority created by decree signed by former President Fernando Henrique
    Cardoso, on June 5, 2001, collegial body with regulatory powers, deliberative
    and consultative, within the respective river basin located in the states of Minas
    Gerais, Goiás, Bahia, Pernambuco, Alagoas, Sergipe and the Federal District.

priority the basin "(BAHIA, 2006, p.12)[97]. Thus, the transposition's water demands (North and East Axis axis) extrapolates the approved water levels, breaking the Ten Year Plan, relevant to the priority uses within environmental sustainability and viability of the project[98].

Even with the mishaps at the time, in April of that same year (2005), a preliminary license installation was granted, valid for one year and with environmental conditions to be fulfilled. Meanwhile, all legal processes and procedures were taking place, products, almost always, the dispute between those interested in the project and those who were opposed or had reservations.

The approval of ANA's opinion, attesting to the availability of water for PISF by CNRH resulted in several protests, one organized by the Manuelzão Project[99], on the 25th of that month during the public hearing of Belo Horizonte. Manuelzão and others promoted a protest that included the symbolic burial of Ministers Ciro Gomes (Integration) and Marina Silva (Environment). Other demonstrations took place simultaneously, in Salvador, Aracaju and Maceio preventing the hearings. Only four of them were held (Pernambuco, Paraíba, Ceará and Rio Grande do Norte). According to the Manuelzão Journal:

97 Bahia Carolina Medeiros (2006), *O Projeto da integração do rio São Francisco às bacias do Nordeste Setentrional e a Lei n. 9433/1997* accessed April 20th 2016 at http://www.scielo.br/pdf/rdgv/v10n2/1808-2432-rdgv-10-2-0497.pdf .

98 "The transposition violates the Ten-Year Plan, it would require, in 2013 at least, a continued flow of 26.4 m³ / s.The use of this flow was postponed to 2015 because of the delay in the original schedule of works. This flow, in itself, goes beyond the actual boundaries of the proposed grantable flow in the plan by 1.4 m³ / s. Nevertheless, according to the grant, the Sustainability Assessment Certificate Hydropower Construction and Technical Note, issued by ANA, may be necessary and granted higher flow rates: 65 m³ / s, 87.9 m³ / s and 127 m³ / s (Henkes). Available at: <http://www.scielo.br/scielo.php?script=sci_arttext&pid=S1808-24322014000200497>.

99 The Manuelzão Project (named after the cowboy Manuel Nardi, immortalized in writing Guimarães Rosa) was created in January 1997 by professors from the initiative of the School of UFMG and aims to "fight for improvements in environmental conditions to promote quality life, breaking with the predominantly paternalistic practice. The river basin of Old Chico was chosen as the focus of activity. " Available at: <http://www.manuelzao.ufmg.br/sobre_o_projeto/historia>.

News outlet Correio Brazilenze and Estado de Minas issued a World Bank study (IBRD) which suggests the project should be rejected. According to the study, the government should seek cheaper projects with another design. On the 14th, the Minister of National Integration, Ciro Gomes was in the show Roda Viva of TV Cultura and answered questions from journalists and professionals who work with the issue of water, including the Manuelzão's coordinator, Apolo Heringer (Revised Manuelzão, 2005, p.14)[100].

There were also demands for the National Congress to check irregularities in the competition notices 1 and 2, from 2005. 27 tax irregularities were found and all have been remedied. In September, the project was released by the Ministry of Integration.

With the legal release, transposition found his greatest opponent, in the comparison of images forces placed in the dynamic scenario. Friar Franciscan Dom Luiz Flávio Cappio went on a hunger strike, which lasted 11 days, starting on 26 September 2005. The chapel of St. Sebastian, in Pernambuco, the bishop demanded to approve the fund for revitalizing the river before the transposition was performed, a requirement that had a favorable opinion of the government. Cappio was not alone, many opposers of the transposition coalesced around. It was the confrontation between the President and former migrant worker *versus* the holy man, both figure had a lot of weight in the northeastern region of Brazil, in a predominantly Catholic country.

In a letter that Dom Cappio sent to President Luiz Inacio Lula da Silva, four points were addressed: "extension of the dialogue, priority revitalization and sanitation of the São Francisco, commitment to the approval of the Proposed Constitutional Amendment (PEC) which would release R$350 million annually for the revitalization of the river, and an audience with the president in Brasilia"[101].

---

100 Magazine Manuelzão (2005), accessed May 14th 2015 at http://www.manuelzao.ufmg.br/assets/files/revista/jornal-30.pdf .

101 Terra Brasil (2005), 'Após dias termina a greve de fome de Dom Cappio', accessed December 20th 2015 at http://noticias.terra.com.br/brasil/noticias/0,OI-697770-EI306,00-Apos+dias+termina+gr%20 eve+de+fome+de+Dom+Cappio.html.

The hearing between the bishop and the president took place. Cappio, in his Letter *Carta Ao Povo do Nordeste*102 (The Northeast People) stated their expectations about the results of that meeting with Lula:

> "When I ended the 11 day fast in Cabrobó, two years ago, I sincerely believed that the federal government would keep its word given in the agreement signed". This agreement established a comprehensive, transparent and participatory national debate on the development of semi-arid and the São Francisco Basin. We believed strongly that if this debate were true the real needs and semiarid potential would be clarified and would be evident that the transposition was not necessary or convenient for the people or the river. The abundant waters of the semiarid would speak for themselves. [...] The government did not fulfill its promise, aborted the debate at its initial stages, won the elections [reelection for president Lula Da Silva] and ordered the army to begin the works of transposition. Movements and organized groups intensified mobilizations and protests, but the government turned a deaf ear to them.

Cappio, believing in the possibility of dialogue, takes the initiative to call the social movements, scholars and NGOs to a meeting in Brasilia in December 2005, which brought together members of the ASA, the Via Campesina, the Landless Rural Workers Movement (MST), of People Affected by Dams Movement (MAB), the Small Farmers Movement (MPA), other representatives of traditional and specialists in the subject communities to discuss a broad and transparent way to build a sustainable development plan based on coexistence with the semiarid region. Interestingly, among these movements are historic allies of the PT governments.

On the current posture of these movements, the Chief Valdecir of Pipipã said that while movements like the MST were present in the initial protests against the transposition, they disappear from the scene, adding that for the landless workers, the land is considered a unit of production, just as the government sees the river just as water

---

102 Dias, Deborah; Castro, Gigi; Said, Magnolia; Gonçalves, Adelaide (Eds.). *A vida por um rio*. Cearense Front For A New Water Culture and against the Transposition of the São Francisco River Waters, Fortaleza.

resource. Unlike the Indians, who establish a much deeper symbolic relationship, sacred to their land and river.

In September (2006), fishermen, boatmen and farmers of the Lower São Francisco area walked 5 km, riding between Sergipe and Alagoas, in protest against "the deterioration of the Old Chico".

> The high point of the manifestation of the riparian happened in the middle of São Francisco in silence, thrilled, they placed the horses in a circle, hands came forward and mounted, promoted a great symbolic embrace to the river. Then they sang hymns in reverence for the life of the Old Chico, threatened by the transposition project of the federal government. [...] The demonstration by the river salvation brought 30 horses and lasted an hour. [...] Among the riverines who participated in the protest ride prevailed tone against the transposition project and in favor of a plan to recover the river. "If you take one more drop of water of our river, he will not withstand it and will die," predicted the fisherman Francis of Assisi, who was keen to participate in the ride to demand for "urgent revitalization of the Old Chico". Miraldo Santos, who also lives off fishing in Brejo Grande, thinks the river situation has worsened in recent years, with disastrous consequences for the population of coastal municipalities. "This area here has given a lot of fish, but today we barely fishing enough to feed the children, imagine to make some money," he reported, in tears[103] .

In early October 2006, recalling one year after the hunger strike of Dom Cappio a camp was organized in Cabrobó (PE), the Truká region, where demonstrations and protests against PISF, walks with leaders and representatives of traditional communities riverside - quilombolas, fishermen, indigenous, tide - among others took place. About 500 people attended the ecumenical act for unification fight for the revitalization of the basin with the participation of dozens of social movements[104]. At that time, the main complaint

---

103 Available at: <http://noticias.ambientebrasil.com.br/clipping/2006/09/13/26765-protesto-no-baixo-sao-francisco-expoe-degradacao-do-rio.html>.

104 In addition to Dom Cappio and Luciana Khoury, representing the Bahia MP, attended the Small Farmers Movement (MPA - AL, SE, PE, BA, PB and national coordination), Landless Workers (MST) and of Dam Affected People (MAB); Pastoral Land Commission (CPT); Council Pastoral dos Pescadores

is against the project item that says "at least 70% of the water will be used for irrigation and only 4% for distribution between the diffused population." Social movements also claimed that while the work continued cracking, the army continued to demarcate and opening paths in the area east of the canal and, moreover, they were beginning to offer compensation to the families who had bee expropriated of the land. Social movements that are against the project realize the political and electoral tone that had been going on since the beginning of the election campaign. The presence of the army, even with the embargoed project showed the sharpness of the decisions taken by the federal government. It demonstrates imposition of force, despite the resounding silence about it in the news media. What you see at most are honorable mentions to the army as the largest most efficient contractor, an incorruptible entity of the country, and its low cost[105] .

In 2007, there was the National Caravan in Rio Protection São Francisco and Semi-Arid, against Transposition. It was composed of eighteen people, including experts and representatives of social movements, ran in thirteen days, eleven capital and four other cities in the northeastern interior, seeking dialogue and pointing alternative solutions for the Brazilian semiarid region.[106]

The Caravan publicly approved and demanded an audience with Lula to present their proposal, which had the support of the Committees of the time (CBH SF) and the roman Catholic Diocese of Barra. However, to everyone's surprise, Don Cappio decided to start on a second hunger strike presenting an ultimatum to the federal government that did not agree with the proposal that had been developed together.

(CPP); Semi-Arid Articulation (ASA), IRPAA, State University of Bahia (UNEB) Articulation of Indigenous Peoples of the Northeast, Minas Gerais and Espirito Santo (APOINME), Indigenous Missionary Council (CIMI) and National Coordination of Rural Black Quilombolas Communities Coordination (CONAQ), among others.

105 Carta Maior (2015), 'Army expedites work in the country and contractors complain', accessed May 22nd 2015 at http://cartamaior.com.br/?/Editoria/ Economia/Exercito-agiliza-obras-no-pais- and-the-contractors up-complain / 7/33329

106 Manuelzão Project (2007), 'The Caravan in defense of São Francisco and the SEMI', accessed May 22nd 2015 at http://www.manuelzao.ufmg.br/ publicacoes/biblioteca_virtual/rio_saofrancisco/saofrancisco_transposicao

The Brazilian Catholic Church was divided in their positions. Don Orani Tempesta of Belém archbishop and president of the Episcopal Commission for Culture, Education and Social Communication of the National Conference of Bishops of Brazil (CNBB), states:

> Geddel knows that the review of the implementation is not unanimous, but we believe in Cappio when he says the government has not complied with the 2005 agreement to open the dialogue. [...] The Church would not want Cappio to make that gesture, but we will never leave him alone[107].

In addition to Archbishop Orani, the president of the CNBB, Dom Geraldo Lyrio and Caritas, an international entity that finances Catholic charities, supported Dom Cappio: «We will not ask him to end the strike, because he has free will. Note that the CNBB is more to supporting Cappio than fasting. He is a good man and he will not be isolated»[108].

On the other hand, minister Geddel Vieira Lima, in a political maneuver, going as far as citing the Catholic band in favor of transposition, reached the point of comparing the attitude of Dom Cappio to a fundamentalist act:

> To trample the rituals, dismiss dialog and ignore the institutions in a democracy is a capital sin. One thing is clear: those who are protesting, are attempting to assault on life itself, and cannot be considered a bishop. He cannot be considered as pastor of a religious flock. He is not a spiritual leader. Cappio's attitude was so publicly condemned by Archbishop Aldo Pagotto, bishop of Paraiba. [...] So Cappio borrowed the symbolic aura of his religious position to put it at the service of political activism based on a fundamentalism that only responds to unconditional surrender. Fundamentalisms, whichever the source, however practiced, are the number one public enemy of democracy. [...] Fundamentalism is all that the church is not, the holy church, my church as an institution. Tolerance and forgiveness have always been sacred pillars of faith, aside with its

---

107 Folha UOL (2007), 'Artigo de Geddel motiva da CNBB a bispo', accessed May 11th 2015 at http://www1.folha.uol.com.br/fsp/brasil/fc1512200725.htm.
108 Idem.

priests devotion because of man who does good. When you see that even political veterans such as former governor Sergipe João Alves Filho, have departed on pilgrimage to take advantage of Cappio's strike, it is clear that the defilement is being used in the attempt of political miracles, through the polls surging numbers. Cappio deserved better apostles. [...] Personally, I have nothing against Cappio. I will always defend the right of citizens like him to express their beliefs. So much so that as soon as I took over the Ministry of National Integration, I called him and asked to dialogue with me. He replied that he would do "some queries" and never returned the call. Cappio sent a letter to the President saying that he would only accept the immediate shut down of the project and archiving project permanently[109].

This time, the Dom Cappio hunger strike reached 23 days and ended with the hospitalization of the bishop in the Intensive Care Unit (ICU) of the Memorial hospital in Petrolina (PE) after fainting while was writing notes about the decision Minister Sepúlveda Pertence on the release of the works of PISF.

Despite the bishop's individual decision, the Caravan decided to support it to save his life, because there was nothing else that could be done. This political option, misguided in the understanding of the organizing direction of the Caravan, played by land the enormous political effort movement that, after the events, was changed to a defensive position.

In the view of Lisboa (2016), the second strike had supported the demands of the Caravan, strengthen the collective work, would have another political significance. But the second strike was one hundred percent counterproductive and ended up isolating the movement.

The result of the second strike was a government reaction to the bishop that undermined all the collective efforts. From there, the government went on the offensive and got an opinion from the Minister Sepúlveda Pertence, annulling all injunctions and releasing the start of the work without the matter had been appreciated on merit, whether the Supreme Court is in Congress.

---

109 Lima, Geddel Vieira (2007), 'O inimigo número 1 da Democracia', Jornal Folha de São Paulo, accessed May 1st 2015 at http://www1.folha.uol.com.br/fsp/opiniao/fz1012200708.htm.

No protest was enough to sustain PISF. In January 2008, the works would resume to promote a discussion on the implementation and some lawmakers and artists who were against it. In April, Dom Cappio pronounced himself completely against PISF, in the 46th Assembly of the CNBB, in Indaiatuba - SP. The debate continues. Roberto Malvezzi[110], the Pastoral Land Commission (CPT) says that, although still unfinished, the channels have directly impacted the environment. According to him, we already see the destruction of the caatinga, surrounding the construction of canals. also denounced the removal of communities that are relocated, or facing major difficulties, as the case of Pipipá Indians, whose territory is crossed by the East Axis channel. The problems of land occupation extends throughout the region where the works are being carried out because the compensation does not always meet the expectations of groups removed to make room for projects.

In June 2011, TCU publishes an audit report[111] which it found possible irregularities in the competition 1/2010 of MI and had the measures the notice of revocation.again there was suspension of the bidding process of the works of PISF, as published in the Unions Official Journal in January 25, 2012[112].

Already in July 2013, anthropologist Manuela Carneiro da Cunha[113], scholar of indigenous issues in the country, accused the management of Dilma Rousseff to promote a development of the facts of "aggressive character" without "barriers that meets imperatives of justice, human rights and conservation." She alerted to the fact we

110 Eco Debate (2015), 'Rio São Francisco: Os impactos da transposição nas comunidades do Semiárido. Entrevista com Roberto Malvezzi, o Gogó', accessed May 14th 2015 at http://www.ecodebate.com.br/2010/04/09/rio-sao-francisco-os-impactos-da-transposicao-nas-comunidades-do-semi-arido-entrevista-com-roberto-malvezzi-o-gogo

111 Court of Audit (2011), 'Audit Report', accessed September 7th 2015 at http://tcu.jusbrasil.com.br/jurisprudencia/316486543/2953920102/inteiro-teor-316486626.

112 Court of Audit (2012), 'Official Gazette', process 037773/2011, accessed April 20th 2015 at http://www.jusbrasil.com.br/diarios/DOU/2012/01/25.

113 Folha UOL (2013), 'Dilma cede a pressão dos ruralistas e rifa os direitos indígenas, diz antropólogo da USP', accessed January 14th 2016 at http://www1.folha.uol.com.br/poder/2013/07/1310677-dilma-cede-a-pressao-dos-ruralistas-e-rifa-os-direitos-indigenas-diz-antropologa-da-usp.shtml>.

watch an unprecedented offensive in Congress against the Indians. The own Attorney General of the Union (AGU), which was ruled by the defense tradition of indigenous rights, allied to the caucus when enacted Ordinance No. 303, a standard that extends to all the marquees, the 19 conditions[114] created by the Supreme Court in the trial of Raposa Serra do Sol in Roraima, a real straitjacket against indigenous people. According to the researcher, "the government gives in to pressure from large farmers and gambles with indigenous rights in exchange for support."

The voice of Dom Luiz Cappio[115] is heard again, it states that the possible new channels, contemplated in the third stage of the CAP would be of an electoral character. In the same momentum of the election year, the drafted bill presented by the Government of Paraiba was approved, to perform a 3rd entry to the waters of the transposition at the entrance of the São Francisco River in Paraíba, the Piancó Valley.

Indigenous struggle: From the "recovery" to the Toré dance

In Brazil today what we see is much more than a "neutralization of native thought." **What you see is a fierce offensive to wipe out the natives,** to sweep their ways of life (and therefore of thought) from the face of the country. What is required today - what we always intended, but today methods are both increasingly subtle and effective without ceasing to be brutal as ever - is to **silence the Indians, disrupt all native thought,** to **turn that caboclada delay,** all that continues to "re-exist" (this is the mode of existence for the Indians

114 Monteiro, Marcela Nogueira (2010), 'O caso raposa Terra do Sol e a jurisprudência do Tribunal Regional Federal da Primeira Região: uma análise do contexto jurisprudencial no qual se insere as 19 cláusulas condicionantes , accessed April 22nd 2015 at http://www.sbdp.org.br/arquivos/monografia/172_Monografia%20Marcela%20Monteiro.pdf.
115 Folha Uol (2013), 'Inacabada, transposição deve ter dois novos eixos' accessed October 14th 2015 at http://www1.folha.uol.com.br/fsp/poder/168630-inacabada-transposicao-deve-ter-dois-novos-eixos.shtml.

in Brazil today: "a resistance")[116] **in poor**, that is, "good Brazilian" badly assisted, barely literate, converted to evangelical Christianity by an army of fanatical missionaries, turned into docile consumer endless supply of junk produced by the world economy. In short: to convert the Indians (those who have not been exterminated before) into 'citizens'. **Poor citizens** of course. A rich Indian would be an almost theological offense, a heresy, the national ideology. **To make it through the Indian poor, you must first take from him what he has - their land, their way of life, ecological and moral foundations of its economy, its internal political autonomy** - to make him want to consume what he doesn't have - which is produced in the land of others (in the country of agricultural business, for example, or the Chinese factories)[117] (Eduardo Viveiros de Castro, 2015) (emphasis added).

Paraiba in 2005 was the Sixth Assembly of the Association of Indigenous Peoples of the Northeast, Minas Gerais and Espirito Santo (APOINME), who referred to the Federal Public Ministry a request the opening of a public civil action to stop the implementation of the river. It claimed that implementation would cause serious harm to the environment in the region and affect at least 25 indigenous people who live on the banks of the river or its tributaries. The APOINME requested in addition to the suspension of the São Francisco Integration Project (PISF), that resources for the work to be transferred to the revitalization of the river.

Signed by various indigenous peoples, among them the Truká and Pipipã, the manifest *Popular Fight debunks the transposition. And keeps going!118* It reveals that for eight days (between June 26 and July 4), the area where the works of PISF were installed was occupied by 1,500 people, linked to social movements to protest the project.

---

116 Note that "rexistir" and "rexistência" consist of a play on words between the pairs 'resist / exist' and 'resistance / existence'.

117 Freitas, Guilherme (2015), 'Eduardo Viveiros de Castro: o que se vê no Brasil hoje é uma ofensa feroz contra os índios', Jornal O Globo, accessed September 3rd 2016 at http://oglobo.globo.com/cultura/livros/eduardo-viveiros-de-castro-que-se-ve-no-brasil-hoje-uma-ofensiva-feroz-contra-os-indios-17261624.

118 Índios Online (2007), 'Luta popular desmascara a transposição', accessed 11th April 2016 at http://www.indiosonline.net/luta_popular_desmascara_a_transposicao/.

The document states that the president of FUNAI acknowledged that the project did not respect indigenous peoples and their territories. To take the struggle forward, the Working Group Truká was created, which could paralyze the actions to remove the water from the Northern Axis and resume a farm in the region. Captained by Truká and peoples of the region, 13 kilometers walked and danced a long toré. At the end of the protest, the demonstrators proclaimed: «the final victory will be when this cruel anti-people project is archived.»

In response to the demonstrations, the minister proposed the creation of a program to bring water to coastal communities, which, although living near the river, remain without continuous supply. Geddel negotiated with the Federal Government to create the Water for All program and inclusion in the Growth Acceleration Program (PAC) in addition to R$300 million addition to the installation of channels, wells and cisterns that would allow the supply of 1,800 riverine communities, approximately 700,000 people. At that time, the cost of implementation of works was valued at R$4.9 billion, excluding spending on the revitalization of the river and social programs related to the project. This minister's solution is revealing given the fact it has been long denounced: the transposition project is not intended to "quench the thirst of the backwoods people," as proclaimed government propaganda, for this to happen, it is necessary to build all that social movements, ASA the locals, always demanded.

Another lawsuit was filed against PISF[119], highlighting the issue of indigenous lands, as the works of PISF were being held in Truká territory, which would require prior approval of Congress. The damage would be irreversible.

---

119 On July 23 , 2008, a direct action of unconstitutionality (ADI) 4113, requesting an injunction, the Supreme Court, in order to suspend the PISF and also Decree No. 5,995 / 2006, arguing that it is unconstitutional because "the normative basis of PISF is undeniably Decree No. 5,995 / 96", which become an "autonomous decree" subject to control by ADI. Another argument was based on breach of the principle of public expenditure efficiency, because the amount of money would benefit only 5% of the northeastern territory and 0.3% of the Brazilian semiarid region population, and disregard other drought-fighting projects considered as most effective and cheap.

In the second half, the APOINME, with the support of several entities[120] produced a report[121], in which indigenous peoples of the Northeast[122] denounce the strong environmental, economic, social and cultural impact in the area of the transposition works of the São Francisco River, which have been neglected by the government, when it denies the negative interference in indigenous, quilombolas and bordering territories. The São Francisco River is critical to the survival of indigenous peoples, essential to agriculture and fisheries held by them. Opará is part of the heritage left by ancestors. Among the impacts of changes, is the defacement of the "cosmological dimension" of the natives, the customs associated with the river, amended to the extent that changes a space that integrates the construction of cultures and worldviews of the inhabitants of the bordering territories by its waters.

In May 2014, there was a visit of President Dilma Rousseff to the work sites of PISF. At that time, the Truká blocked the BR-428 in protest against the transposition[123] but were prevented from reaching the venue. Without waiting, they descended from the buses and continued walking to a point where they were barred. With posters and banners, protesters charged the promised investments in education, program incentives MCMV and a pier for mooring the

---

120 The APOINME had the support of OXFAM / European Union Project Articulation People for Revitalization of the São Francisco and Project New Cartography of Traditional Peoples and Communities of Brazil's São Francisco (UFAM / NECTAS / UNEB), and had as allies the Bar Association of Rural Workers in the State of Bahia (AATR), the Study Group on Communities and Traditional and Social and Environmental Actions Peoples (NECTAS / UNEB), the Pastoral Council of Fishermen / NE (CPP) and the Indian Council missionary (CIMI).

121 CIMI complaint Report (2007), 'Indigenous people affected with the transposition of the São Francisco River, accessed September 15th 2015 at http://www.cimi.org.br/pub/publicacoes/1241549933_relatapoinmetransp.pdf.

122 Ethnic Truká, Tumbalalá, Pankararu, Anacé, Tuxá, Pipipã, Kambiwá, Xoco and Kariri-Xoco, located in the states of Bahia, Pernambuco, Sergipe, Alagoas and Ceará.

123 JC Online (2014), 'Durante visita de dilma, indígenas da tribo Truká bloqueiam BR 428 em protesto', accessed October 20th 2015 at http://jconline.ne10.uol.com.br/canal/politica/pernambuco/noticia/2014/05/13/durante-visita-de-dilma-indigenas-da-tribo-truka-bloqueiam-br-428-em-protesto-127856.php.

São Francisco River, that was promised in 2011 by the Minister of National Integration.

And how did these two people resist? There were very few Pipipá contacts, but if you could visit their territory and interview its leaders. Of them, little is known, since there is little reference in academic literature.

By interviewing a Chief, it was learned that Pipipá joined other groups, indigenous and non-indigenous, the transposition resistance, including pointing out, the abandonment of certain non-indigenous social movements like the MST. There are testimonials, as Benedito (May, 2016) expressing disbelief in the struggle of the Pipipá:

> [...] There are people who got angry, really angry [with the transposition] right? But what could we have done? [...] But here no one has done anything ... people are too slow, right? This is why people suffer, right? Because ... because we are not aggressive enough to ... we're too stupid, is not it? Sure ... because other people would had done anything, any aggression there, but no... some are dying on silence just fighting, fighting, but there nothing to do, right?

Anyway, these two unique voices were the feeling of helplessness before interests, overwhelming, state and associates, that transposition represents.

Truká already have a tradition of previous fights to transposition, the "recoveries". They are instruments not only to reclaim the land, as well as affirmation of ethnic identity. From 1981 to 2007, there were five "recoveries". Taken over these have always been peaceful actions, trying to give visibility to their claims for land or so left of violence by the state, faced arrests and some of its leaders were killed by the police.

According to the report of Chief Neguinho, the Truká youth was present in the fight for people's rights, since the 1990s, the first "recoveries". The participation of young people in religious groups and the relationship with people of CIMI and later the Cultural Center Luiz Freire encouraged young people, many of them children of leaders, to engage in the lands struggles, becoming important in decisions and intrusion actions land[124].

---

124 About the indigenous movement in northeastern see OLIVEIRA, KE, 2013.

The recovery of Bica, the last in possession of the whole territory of the island in 1999, a group of committed young people created the OJIT - Youth Organization Indigenous Truká. The organization was active during the recovery of Bica, but eventually institutionally undid after a prolonged the recovery in Farm Antonio Lalinha, near the city of Cabrobó in 2007. That last recovery, positioned themselves contrecoveriesary to the government's imposition of performing the transposition works of the São Francisco and were repressed by the military and federal police. In contrast, Truká held a protest in the form of walking, dancing the Toré.

> There is the question of youth. 2007 for issues of this fight, the São Francisco river transposition, the occupation of a large territory that belongs to Truká. Neguinho mobilized with large indigenous community to block this transposition. We had that whole question of ... the police with a lot of people ... were one month camped there in Tucutu saw that there is also traditional land of the indigenous people, Truká. At the same time the federal police came here and arrested me for the sake of the land, the fight for the land ... then a few days I was released from justice, went to fight again. (Pajé Adilson).

Over time, these young men became parents, and leaders, being replaced by new Truká, what went to call the joint youth. The new generation, that same year, created the theater group. Two plays were produced by them, one of them talking about the need to care for the environment and the other on the history of their people. The theater work is done with great effort and almost without resources, always politicized and inserted into the indigenous movement. The group's activities corresponded to engage these young people in a movement of political and identity connotation. The themes of her two unique pieces make it an evident concern with the environment and reproduction of its people, already influenced by the moment lived by them the impact that the river has suffered, but also deforestation of the savannah in the territory, the problem with waste, improper cultivation of some crops, salinization of the land.

Considering the temporal arch located between the beginning of the transposition works of the São Francisco River, simultaneously the last recovery of the farm Lalinha Antonio, started in 2007[125], and the year 2016, it is clear that part of the indigenous youth who participated in these struggles, is still at work in the indigenous movement in the state of Pernambuco.

Indigenous teachers talked about the threats that the Truká suffer, in the booklet that produced *No Reino da Assunção, Reina Truká* (In the Kingdom of Assunção, Reigns Truká) (p.41): "As we have seen so far, since colonization that our land was being invaded... The Brazilian state, which should protect us, because the land is ours by right, was exactly who most threatened us through the military and federal police."

The leaders, the indigenous school and the theater are organized ways to keep the memory of these struggles alive, to discuss the transposition. They are the bases for organization of struggles and rights of conquest narratives.

In addition to resistance to face alone or almost alone, the Truká associated with other groups, indigenous or not, in the fight against the transposition, in the fight for the revitalization of the river. Since 2005, they participated in meetings with other indigenous, quilombolas and riverine groups in relation to the transposition[126].

Over the years, the media silences, to know as little as possible about new rush of Truká against these injustices that accumulate over the recent times.

---

125 Antropozoide (2007), 'recapture do povo indígena Truká: em busca da homologação contínua', July 23rd, accessed May 20th 2015 at http://antropozoide. blogspot.com.br/2007/07/recente-retomada-truk-oficializada-no.html.
126 CIMI complaint Report (2007), 'Indigenous people affected with the transposition of the São Francisco River, accessed September 15th 2015 at http://www.cimi.org.br/pub/publicacoes/1241549933_relatapoinmetransp.pdf.

Conclusion: Another look at life on Earth: a civilization without transpositions

If a living, free-flowing river is a good thing to have on this planet, Then it is good independently of human existence and interests, and it would equally be a good thing on the planet that never hosted conscious life.[127]

Civilized people are accustomed to an anthropocentric view of the world. Our interest in the environment is utilitarian: it is of value because it is of use to human beings - if only as a place for camping and recreation.
Primitive and eco-centric worldviews are incalculable. At present, we human Beings - while considering ourselves the most intelligent species on the planet - are engaged in the most unintelligent enterprise imaginable: the destruction of our own natural life-support system [...] it seems unlikely that these could ever have arisen but for an entrenched and peoples, in contrast, tend to see the intrinsically meaningful nature [...]
The difference in effects between the anthropocentric deepening trend of thinking que separates humanity from its natural context and denies inherent worth to non-human nature ...*128*

In the year 2015, when the stone barrier that separated the São Francisco river transposition of the canal was blown up, the waters entered the concrete channel. This view has produced a sense of the end of a time, the defeat of those who fought against the execution of this work.

---

127 Environmental Ethics (2016) The Debate Over Anthropocentrism, accessed October, 9th 2016 at http://science.jrank.org/pages/9156/Environmental-Ethics-Debate-over-Anthropocentrism. html.
128 Heinberg, Richard (1997), "Was Civilization a Mistake?" in *Green Anarchist*, Autumn.

For almost 10 years, there was a clash between two world views, river, relationship with nature and, above all, a clash between different priorities: to preserve and restore the river and degraded forests over the centuries, or invest in needs agricultural businesses and growth.

Today, in the last quarter of 2016, the waters remain in the channel, waiting to be pumped, to take the enchanted waters to the distant fields to irrigate the fields of agricultural business and fill the fetid pools of shrimp farming. What will be the fate of the river after this contract? The theme takes up little space in the media, except for the disclosure of the release of funds for revitalization to be held by the new government. There is little enthusiasm perhaps little belief about these plans.

In this book, we told the story of the project, we exposed the different positions, and against its realization, informed in different worldviews, life, nature and the supernatural world. Here is the existing asymmetrical power in the clash between the groups who advocated opposing positions. It was a negotiation between unequals, in which one side imposed their interests, wishes and views using many means of persuasion by force, whether by law or weapons.

The fight against the construction of transposition brought to the scene friction between two realities that are intertwined, but remain set apart from each other. Unequal worlds. One imagines they won, leaving a devastation mark and walking over everything that was valuable and sacred to the defeated, those who do not see the river as a mere water resource. Among the losers are those who understand that the river is a living being, where there is a world that keeps mysteries, so the river is a sacred element. Not only traditional people, environmentalists and others who participated in this struggle have this perception of the river and its uses are incompatible with the vision of a mere water resource. In fact, they clashed with different environmental ethics.

But in what ways does the Indians worldview of the remote Hinterlands coincide with scientists from prestigious universities in the country, environmental activists, pastoral agents, prosecutors members, fishermen, field movements? That perceptions do they share that government's desires for economic growth are faced so radically? Yes, because it is in the name of growth, incessant production of wealth that supposedly mitigate the misery of the country that everything would become acceptable and justifiable.

If not for the inclusion of scientists and activists, those unaware could understand that it is a clash between the rural past and pre-modern and the future civilization, whose roots are in the urban and industrial society. However, it is a false perception, the resistance is not an expression of an agrarian world stagnated against the advances of industrial modernity in the field and the benefits promised by it.

What has been questioned, for decades, is the industrial and civilization model, incompatible with human and planetary needs of the twenty-first century. In a country like Brazil, left and right wing policies differ in society projects, however, they do not abdicate from industrialism as the production source of society's wealth and growth. Parties and ideologies, even the most antagonistic ones, accept the idea that "all economic growth is good." In this regard, the fascists and leftist extremists act as faces of the same coin, conjoined twins.

The Industrial Revolution brought a sense of economy that revolves around the incessant growth idea. Industrialism can be adopted by any production mode serves to capitalist production as well as socialist. The big difference was in the ownership of means of production, or in the hands of the ruling class, or in the state (which does not seem like a big difference!), and the distribution of wealth, which would supposedly is more just in socialism ensuring that the results of growth are shared. However, the history of the world does not have in situations that there is, indeed, been satisfying.

Since the Rio 92, politicians, activists and scholars warn of the fact that the passport to the future, the gateway to the celebrated modernity, reclaims from countries such as Brazil, the conservation of 'natural resources': mangroves, basins , rivers, seas, forests, fields... because, despite its use condition, it does comply the homeostatic function, maintaining the planetary balance within acceptable standards to life forms.

The inclusion of Brazil in the select club of 'civilized/rich' countries would aid the preservation of what is left of their overworked nature. Ironically, it is necessary to rescue that nature which, since colonial times, it is tried to be destroyed to build a civilization. Now, that is the price charged to be accepted as part of the same civilization.

Obviously, the rich countries that are charging us are not questioning industrialism, let alone failing to invest in the production of wealth. However, they need to respond to the internal pressures of political groups demanding a new direction of the economy and politics for ecological preservation. Since the 1970s, these environmental groups and pacifists increased pressure in Europe and North America.

Among them, the decrement movement that is expanding throughout the world, and with it, the concept of sustainable development that, in 1987, was still palatable, now has a different connotation. It became a concept emptied in essence, to the extent that plays the same bureaucratic and management solutions that led us to the current environmental crisis.

What is decrement?

Let's face it : in fact we do not have a plan B, because there is no plan B.[129]

A basic assumption is that any savings there from a physical environment depends on the continuous use of natural resources such as water, forests, agricultural land, resources, renewable or not, which are produced in limited quantities due to the environment's capacity to regenerate them.

At the same time, when the production system produces waste faster than the ability to absorb nature, it overwhelms the capacity of the planet to sustain its existence. Today, the calculation is that humanity consumes almost 30% above the biosphere regenerative capacity[130].

Currently, we make use of resources on a higher level than the natural renewal capacity and produce waste faster than nature can absorb. If we continue with this kind of economic growth, the pressure on the planet will collapse. Keeping the planet alive requires a reformulation of economies, so suited to the limits imposed by the

---

129 Nabarro, David (2016), 'Conselheiro especial de Ban Ki-moon para a Agenda de Desenvolvimento Sustentável 2030', *Folha de São Paulo*, September 2016.
130 Latouche, S. (2009) *Pequeno Tratado do Decrescimento Sereno*, São Paulo, WMF Martins Fontes.

physical environment. That is, a limited earth where resources are limited and incompatible with unlimited growth. All beings on Earth need to consume natural resources in order to live. However, surviving on a living planet implies the consumption within the limits of natural boundaries, as waste must have a volume that nature can absorb. Keeping the planet alive requires a better balance between the use and abuse of nature.

Nicholas Georgescu-Roegen[131] in 1971, was the creator of the bioeconomy. It was the decade of the Club of Rome, of the Stockholm Conference and many doomsday predictions, of the zero-growth club. The author problematized the relationship between the law of entropy and the economic processes which, for him, would jeopardize the survival of life on Earth. Later in 1975, he dubbed the term decrement[132] as the process to follow so as to achieve a development model that was sustainable.

In the same vein, Herman Daly[133] proposes that the economy remains in a state of transition to reach a steady state, the adoption of a scale of production that does not exceed the carrying capacity is required of ecosystems. The radical change of focus of the economy would be the only way to achieve sustainable development[134].

The move beyond the borders of the Anglo-Saxon world, earns other adepts as Besson-Girad[135], Aries[136], thinkers and activists engage the de-growth discussion as a concrete proposal, incorporating on the platforms to overcome the crisis of industrial society, propose a change in civilizational character in all directions: economic, political, cultural, ecological and spiritual.

131 Raine, Alan, Foster, John, Potts, Jason (1971), 'The Entropy Law and the Economic Process', *Ecological Complexity*, accessed September, 14 2016 at http://www.sciencedirect.com/science/article/pii/S1476945X07000104.

132 Georgescu- Roegen, Nicholas (1975), La décroissance: Entropie – Écologie – Économie, Paris: Éditions Sang de la terre.

133 Daly, Herman E. (1977) *Steady- Economics*, Washington, DC: Island Press.

134 Daly, Herman E. (1996), *Beyond Growth: The Economics of Sustainable Development*, Boston: Beacon Press.

135 Besson-Girad, Jean-Claude (2005), *Decrescendo Cantabile: Petit Manuel pour une décroissance harmonique*, Lyon: Paragon.

136 Áries, Paul (2005), *Décroissance ou barbárie*, Paris: Editions Golias.

As per Latouche[137] (2009) a society was built of exclusion, inequality, poverty, environmental devastation, and we face the serious threat of global warming. This unsustainable society model should be replaced by another in which public policies are democratic, participatory and lifestyle adopted are of conscious consumption.

Latouche observes the capitalist system to criticize his society that is being absorbed by an economy whose sole purpose is growth for the sake of growth... However, this is the premise of industrial society, whether capitalist or not, it is to produce, incessant growth despite purposes.

Decrement is not the same thing as negative growth. It is understood that the decrement in growth brings unemployment, poverty and uncertainty for companies, compromising spending on key items for social and environmental well-being. For Latouche, decrement is a possible utopia, a proposal, a political project that will allow a better life. The concept of decrement is not unrealistic, but seeks objective possibilities for its application, to establish itself as a societal project. The author presents in his proposal a concrete formula to enter this "virtuous circle" of serene decrease from the adoption of eight interdependent mutually reinforcing changes: reevaluate, re-conceptualize, restructure, redistribute, relocate, reduce, reuse, recycle (Latouche, 2009, p. 42).

In this perspective, the author suggests the decrement to the southern hemisphere, including countries with great poverty, as this would cause a spiraling motion to enter the orbit of the virtuous circle of the eight "R's" (Latouche, 2009, p. 81) and the from there, it would be possible to break the economic dependence of the North and, in the case of Africa, it also would include the Chinese industrialism.

The decrement is a movement spread around the world that stands as anti-system and proposes a paradigm of radical change to the structural crisis of modern and highly technologized society. It brings a proposal of individual and collective change because it is based on a new relationship with the environment and with all kinds of life.

The idea of the living planet recognizes that technological advances do not have the power to allow us to continue growing indefinitely.

---

137 Latouche, S. (2009) *Pequeno Tratado do Decrescimento Sereno*, São Paulo, WMF Martins Fontes.

Technology does not create something from nothing. Technology does not change the fact that there is a limited amount of resources in a world with more people and, consequently, increased consumption. If the increase in technological efficiency can make you gain more time, these gains will be fatally canceled by continued growth.

We reached the point of no return, where we face two possibilities: either credit the power to reverse the damage done to the life of the planet to technology; or abandon the obsessive idea of infinite growth on a finite planet, otherwise we will be renewing the premise of the Jevons Paradox[138].

If technological advances accelerate communication, mobility etc., they can, however, act as sources of exploitation and alienation, especially when the monopoly of science and technology is concentrated in the hands of few, whose priorities are not, and never were, the life on the planet.

The decrement theory anchors a movement fighting to make the use of the planet occurs in a sustainable manner ensuring a future resilience. For this, it seeks to strengthen sustainable social and ecological practices that recognize the physical limits of the Earth.

If the unlimited growth has always been the keynote of industrialism, in recent decades, globalization accelerated this process to unsustainable. The orientation for growth, increasingly, leads to changes in the relationship between humans and nature.

The human condition in technologized society generates an immense dissatisfaction, disbelief in economic systems and solutions offered by traditional policies. In the midst of this dissatisfaction, other perspectives emerge around the globe, people are looking for new possibilities and embrace ideas like the decrement. Because it was clear that if the pursuit of continued growth brought any advantage, it was at the expense of people and the natural environment, increased inequality, preying of non-renewable resources, pollution, caused the extinction of plants and animals brought insecurity, sense of loss of community and is already threatening the Earth's capacity to

138 The paradox of Jevons (/ dʒɛvənz / or Jevons effect) occurs when technological progress increases efficiency with which a resource is used, but the rate of consumption of that resource increases due to increased demand. The Jevons paradox should be the paradox of the most widely known ecological economics.

support us. Understanding this scenario brought a relevant question: what can we do without economic growth?

The decrement or post-growth functions as an umbrella that shelters several emerging perspectives, new ways of seeing the world that suggest overcoming growth. They all point to a multiplicity of possible futures, or even to rescue lifestyles that exist in other societies. They all share the desire to have a healthy growth in which human potential can be developed without compromising the ends of the earth. The post-growth economy, in any of its variants, puts life at the center of economic and social activity.

None of this will be possible without a new understanding of nature, because we cannot continue treating the gifts of nature as a commodity to use and dispose of, decrement involves treating the world as an ecosystem to grow.

A society, by adopting decrement can define multiple forms of economy, depending on the available resources, history and culture of the people and of the vocation of each region.

According Bocato-Franco (2013), the movement by decreasing the target of frequent criticism. The main one tries to present it as a *neomalthusian* movement, as the decrement suggests that the population and the global consumption are stabilized or reduced. The fact is that a decrease, a reduction of the population, or even its regulation, can only be decided in a democratic and equitable manner in which the role of women is crucial because it is up to her and her only (never to man, state or church) to decide whether or not to have children, when to have them and the amount of the offspring, the bet is much more in the emancipation, empowerment and active participation of women than in violent and authoritarian proposals advocated by Malthus.

Another common criticism of decrementalists is that the movement would be nostalgic in the search for a pre-civilizational lifestyle, against technology and progress. Before asking exactly what progress and for whom? It is noteworthy that the movement is very broad, as we have explained, it encompasses numerous groups. This criticism would make more sense if it were addressed to Primitivism, a specific group, which may or may not integrate the movement for Decrement in some places.

> Currently, numerous collective practical experimentation, discussion groups, research and train in countries of North and South,

including Brazil that self-recognize as part of the movement for Decrement. All the methods and knowledge are contributing to the construction of multiple identities and understanding on decrement [...] So this is a movement still in formation and significance process.(Bocato-Franco, 2013)[139].

Meanwhile, in the tropics ...

If the Decrement movement opens up the possibility to rethink civilization in more environmentally sustainable terms and more satisfactory inter-human relations in Brazil we continue to degrade the land as much as possible, polluting rivers where water is scarce, tearing down and burning forests. Our citizenship is not refined enough to extend the idea of rights to inanimate nature, or the forms of non-human life. We suffer from acute anthropocentrism. The fear is that when we achieve this level of environmental awareness, there will no longer be anything to preserve.

To the extent that we are violent to nature, we lose the sense of community, and solidarity dissolves in a frayed social fabric. Violence increases in frightening proportions, even after the implementation of social inclusion programs that seem to have no impact on the reduction of violence. On the contrary to some expectations of doctrines credited to fair economic distribution solution to all problems of mankind.

The political upheaval that occurred in the country in the year 2016, the replacement of political leaders does not seem to have caused any change in the implementation of the project of the São Francisco River. In the words of the Ministry of Integration, asked about the possibility of reconciling work of transposition with the revitalization of the river, they argue that:

> More possible, is needed. The Integration Project of the São Francisco River, vital to the population Ceará, Paraíba, Pernambuco and Rio Grande do Norte, depends on the availability of water in ade-

---

139 Bocato-Franco, Alan, (2013), Para Compreender o Decrescimento, Carta Capital, accessed November 5th 2016 at http://www.cartacapital.com.br/blogs/outras-palavras/para-compreender-o-201cdecrescimento201d-3687.html

quate quantity and quality. The actions taken for the Revitalization guarantee water resources for future generations[140].

We asked what will project New Chico do. They claim that this is a "new phase for the revitalization, in which the action will be continuous, with a long-term vision and approach between the planning and activities of the different actors, public and private"[141].

And although the new Chico Plan and the new phase of the Revitalization Program:

> [...] They are not designed to differentiate the previous management. It is a new concept that the river needs a long-term state intervention, which pervades administrations, parties and people. The main difference between the new and the previous phase was precisely designed by a governance system between different instances[142].

The statements confirm that there is no differentiation between the previous administration and the current. The new government did not condemn the work of its predecessors, by the way, once 85% of the path is complete, it would be almost impossible at this point, to reverse the damage that it caused, and at best, with good will -it can minimize the negative effects on the environment and affected populations.

However, even without condemning it, the new government, in the words of the Ministry of Integration also takes this project as:

> The work is necessary for the receiving basins "to reach a guaranteed water supply, which require a flow rate of 26.4 m³/s (flow that the current grant allows pump). However, the São Francisco Project is able to pump up to 127 m³/s, which is only possible with more favorable water conditions, which is the Revitalization Program's goal[143].

---

140 Advisory Communication of the Ministry of National Integration, personal communication, September 2016
141 Idem.
142 Idem.
143 Idem.

Revitalization of São Francisco: Only a civilizing Shock[144]

"Necessary? Could it be? Is that right, Professor Apolo? Tell us. Enlighten us, clarify on this 'official truth'."
Apolo Heringer Lisboa[145], founder and coordinator of the 2007 Caravan in defense of São Francisco, the semi-arid and Against Transposition.

When the federal government announced the New Chico project to support the transposition, we then concluded: They must believe the Old Chico resources are running out and are thinking of creating an artificial river, a new Chico!

How is the basin today? Old Chico appeared on Earth, in today's path, for millions of years. Its ecosystems are fully supported, photosynthesis, producing food and conserving *habitat* for all living beings, without waste or sewage, everything is recyclable. It was an example of fully sustainable natural or ecologic economy. Has culture brought in politics and the economy to prioritize things that nature was already able to do so well on its own? This is a fundamental question to be answered by the current economic authorities.

It is interesting to note that the extreme upper and lower parts of the Rio São Francisco (RSF) have good rainfall, while its mid and sub-medium traverses severe semiarid climate areas. It is a basin with an approximate area of 640,000 square kilometers and 2830 kilometers (km) long, in its main channel. About 75% of runoff of São Francisco is generated in Minas Gerais, whose inserted basin area is only 37% of the total area. The area between the border Minas-Gerais and Bahia the city of Juazeiro (BA) already represents 45% of the valley area and contributes to only 20% of the annual runoff of the basin. A great strategic value of information is, then, that the states

---

144 Text produced by Apolo Heringer Lisboa with the essential contribution of Professor José do Patrocínio Tomaz Albuquerque, Federal University of Campina Grande (UFCG) and chemical engineer, former employee of Petrobras, Francisco de Assis Pereira, both of Morrinhos Charter group.

145 At http://www.apoloheringerlisboa.com/ CV: http://lattes.cnpq.br/ 8584595137405086 Facebook: https://www.facebook.com/apoloheringerlisbo

of Minas Gerais and Bahia account for 82% of the basin area of São Francisco and 95% of the water yielded, meaning the totality of the river water.[146]

Sobradinho/BA, where the great dam was built for hydroelectric production, is located on the border with Pernambuco, Petrolina region, and a unique role in the *management* of the river was acquired, since its opening at the end of the 1970s. Sobradinho can store a total volume of 34 billion m^3 of water with a useful volume of 28 billion m^3, a vast expanse of approximately 350 km by 10-40 wide, semi-arid climate with colossal evaporation of approximately 250 mm/ second on average. It is a rain from the bottom up! In recent years, Sobradinho has approached the dead volume at the end of the dry season, bringing to our memory the hydro-blackout of 2001. Strong concerns are overtaking of the whole basin of the São Francisco river from September until December.

In this scenario, the routine of farmers is to observe the movement of clouds and the cicadas' singing; meteorologists provide data and make reports; agricultural businesses calculates the water reserves, flow rates of wells and already fear a collapse; the hydroelectric sector discusses whether to turn on the heat; fishermen observe the lagoons dry without being able to count on the great floods that that exceptionally reset its life cycle . This pre-bankruptcy condition of the São Francisco river questions the way it has been treated, since the colonial times, the so-called River of National Integration. The Three Marias reservoir can store 19 billion m^3, total volume and useful volume of 15 billion. Increased defluence in Tres Marias to respond Sobradinho, brings an ephemeral tranquility along the middle course of the São Francisco river, but generating tensions surrounding the Lake of Tres Marias, which tends to approach the dead volume, even without providing guarantees firm to Sobradinho. But to respond with half measures, with its ecosystems and its people, has never been the main objective of these operations in the dams. Everything is done in the authoritarian logic of the powerful hydroelectric system, under the command of the National Electric System Operator (ONS), which is now being forced to share their power with irrigation because of the political power of big agricultural business

---

146 At https://pt.wikipedia.org/wiki/Rio_S%C3%A3o_Francisco

lobby in Congress. The ONS and the National Water Agency (ANA), try to *manage* the basin with immediate objectives, economistic and source of inputs. But no formal conventional planning achieves good results. We reserve the term *managing* the most demanding and complex sense of comprehensive treatment and integrated nature. With this kind of management, there is no concern with the ecosystem aspects of the basin, natural source *sine qua non* of water conservation. A river is not a single channel water that flows for economic purposes of certain social classes. The dominant economic sector is indifferent to widespread deforestation and does not see the relationship between ecosystems, biodiversity, soil, water, people and economy. It does not attach importance to the survival of marginal lagoons of the gutter and tributaries, vital to the richness of the fish fauna of the basin. The water crisis, not to soil conservation, the complex network problems with pesticides, monocultures, the social crisis, which endures and is generated, are external phenomena seen as inevitable to hydroelectric interests, industrial, mining and agricultural business. They work with the rationality of corporations and lavish financial and political incentives to circumvent environmental and legal limits. Meanwhile, water insecurity is establishing itself as consolidated and growing trend in which acute attacks have been repeated in increasingly shorter periods.

And the implementation of water has not started and therefore cannot be held responsible for the transposition of the current water crisis. Neither the main problem of the origin can be charged to the periodic lack of rain, as the dams of Três Marias and Sobradinho were built aiming to meeting and solving the planned demand with 100% guarantee, taking into account the weather and historical data droughts. But, in the end of 2015, an emergency project required direct intervention of the presidency to install a floating bomb that could bring dead volume water from the lake to the great project of Nilo Coelho irrigation. The production of electricity ceased during this period.

This imbalance occurred when the federal government between Dec/2012 and Jan/2013, already in full force of the current drought, put the hydroelectric cascade turbines of the Hydroelectric Company of São Francisco (Chesf) to run at full capacity to prevent a black out energy on the Southeast region, which could have a devastating effect on the 2014 presidential elections. By doing so, he emptied

Sobradinho. Now, in an attempt to leave the suffocating situation and reverse the framework installed, the federal government and the ONS appeals to oracles, crossing the fingers for abundant rainfall to come and the previous levels to be recovered by restoring the regulatory role of Sobradinho. At the same time, they find themselves forced to reduce the flow defluence of Sobradinho each year, affecting the hydropower system installed, transport by ferries, canoes and human supply of cities downstream from Sobradinho to the Ocean. They are great losses for Brazil. In 2016, forecasts were more critical than the realities of 2015 and 2014.

The transposition will only enlarge the crisis in its territory. The expectation of economic growth for the water supply of São Francisco to the northern Northeast will produce in this great region, a demographic swelling induced poles of growth and new water demands. It will be a demand with more unsustainable use of the waters of São Francisco, pressing Sobradinho, whose flow of current defluence, something around 840 m³/s, is more than 50% below its regularization evaluated flow, based on a number of tributaries streamflow data Sobradinho in 1715 m³/s for technical ANA (Sousa Freitas Gondim & Son, 2004). This flow, now used, does not meet the human needs of coastal cities and even less ecological, which needs 1,300 m³/s. The absurdity of the decision in favor of the São Francisco river Transposition, larger project of the Growth Acceleration Program (PAC), followed the path of deadly political relationship of corruption among the federal government, contractors and political parties, to be contextualized in the following paragraphs.

It is clear that the transposition was not necessary nor advisable, both hydraulically and financially. The way it is being done, it is a technical fraud involving political aspirations involving cement, steel, construction companies, political parties interests and the power to project the federal government installed in 2003. For the sake of truth, it should be noted that, with the support of PT, strong mobilization of public opinion and with the support of the then Minister of the Environment, José Carlos Carvalho, could, at the end of the Fernando Henrique Cardoso government, archive the Transposition project, which Lula brought back in 2003 at the beginning of his term, even though he was against it during the election campaign 2002!

If the government's true objective were for human supply, watering animals, small farmers and family economy and small farmers, if and when the North Northeast needed, of course, the work would be done with closed tubes and not through open channels, making all the difference costs, operation and losses related to evaporation.

Contrary to what was announced by marketers, it is not the project carried out with the aim of bringing a glass of water to the thirsty. This is the largest PAC investment to meet agricultural business demand with very demanding projects in water consumption, an abomination in terms of the semiarid region, which has a wonderfully flora and fauna adapted to the climate. The natural intelligence of this adaptation is an essential resource to claim a regional agricultural economy and sustainable animals, and fully viable to export highly appreciated and valued native products. The semi-arid hinterland is rich in flora and fauna that the discourse of the dry industry has failed to appreciate because the political and parasitical crying of the Republic yielded more without the need to invest and work.

According to recent information we have, the Office of Communications of the Ministry of National Integration (MIN), "the work is necessary for receiving basins to achieve water security, which require a flow rate of 26.4 m³/s (flow that currently allows the use of the pump). However, the São Francisco Project is able to pump up to 127 m³/s, which is only possible with more favorable water conditions, which is a goal of the Revitalization Program." Consultants state, that the New Chico project is a result of the governments belief that the São Francisco river needs of the Brazilian state intervention. Now, would they be nationalizing the damage caused by the market? New Chico means investments in infrastructure, with public financing to the private sector, which is not paid by the gross water use. We show forth as the issue is regarding payment for water in the São Francisco basin, as per ANA data.

The work was oversized, with huge costs in electricity, maintenance and personnel. Absurd, according the unsuspected engineer from Ceará, former director of the National Department of Works Against Drought (DNOCS), Cássio Borges, who was in favor of transposition. According to his report, the oversized work will have to run at 100% of the time, for technical reasons of conservation

123

equipment such as electric pumps, tunnels, canals, maintenance, all this resulting in high energy operating costs, water and personnel. We received the distinguished engineer's email, summarizing views made public in his state:

> [...] I request measures by the authorities in order ... to avoid, at all costs, which created a new institution to be the manager of the São Francisco River Integration Project. Before any other consideration in this regard, I must say that I consider foolish the creation of this new body that will only act or operate 40% of the time in our region. Just as a quick analysis of rainfall data from FUNCEME, these past seven years, to conclude that since 2003 the state of Ceará, taking this as an example, would not have needed, as it indeed did not, from the São Francisco River waters. I see no need to create a new body in our region, as we already have DNOCS with all its experience, experience with the semi-arid, administrative structure, technical and operational deployed in the area of this enterprise. (Eng. Cássio Borges, on September 29, 2011).

As proposed by the Atlas of Brazil, ANA, the distribution of water should be prioritized, existing in large dams in the region, to the small towns and villages lacking water. The large and medium reservoirs are federal public works, built from the beginning of the twentieth century, these salinization processes by evaporation and without full usefulness, which are close to the land of large landowners.

We can say that the misery of the Northeast is not for lack of water, because if so, in regions with more water there would be no misery. Today, unlike the time of the paintings of Portinari on refugees, there was a high urban concentration and the water supply was easier. Extended to income distribution policies as family assistance program, pensions and severance packages in rural areas, improvement in communication infrastructures, transportation, healthcare and education, which took the drama of the ancient scourge so well exploited by the mafia drought industry in the Northeast. But this menacing specter was abused by the drought industry secularly installed in the Northeast by the colonels of politics. Their version prevailed in Brasilia on the technical and scientific advice of the cream of the national hydrology.

We know that the transposition project was the result of Lula's political agreement with Ciro Gomes in the second round of election in 2002 to address the dispute with José Serra. Thus, the PT changed its previous position and appointed as Minister Marina Silva, who was against the project, to take care of their approval and licensing.

When the federal government passed a judgment authorizing the water grant for the Transposition decision "technique" of ANA, it was generated in the basin of São Francisco, the race for water with the conquest of guarantors grants of various irrigation projects and supply in various states of São Francisco basin. It was a form of cowardly, regionalist and unpatriotic resistance to the Transposition project, sowing pumps for the future, the prospect of a fierce dispute over water between states of the Brazilian federation. There was flurry of lack of support policy grants for technical analysis, which have pointed to the water deficit in the donor basin with best land and the existence of other best proposals for the Northern Northeast, present in hydrologists publications such as Aldo Rebouças, Jose do Patrocinio Tomaz Albuquerque Manoel Bomfim and others. The authorization Transposition was a service through autocratic decision of the Minister Sepúlveda, who belongs to the Supreme Court, annulling the contrary injunctions, without the Supreme Court having manifested the merits, as well as the National Congress, after years of disputes between states. It worked like a charm in favor of the darker side of Brazil, stabbing national interests in favor of corruption.

The official and business version which meets the requirements of popular and political common sense gives the depletion of regulatory capacity of Sobradinho and the severity of drought, prolonged droughts, referring to the lack of rain. Of course, if it rained all the time, an anomaly of nature, the runoff would keep the rivers with water permanently, there would be no seasonal rivers. But the idea of lack of rain is only half true. The predictable cyclic variation, based on historical series, is what determines the size of the dam and the volume to be stored to ensure the water supply provided with 100% guarantee.

Explaining the huge expansion of agricultural business in the Brazilian *Cerrado* policy made further possible by soil research and new technologies, expanding agriculture and livestock production to meet the international demand for *commodities,* it is very demanding on water. There was widespread deforestation of the *Cerrado* and a strong wave of drilling deep wells that reach 700 meters deep, and dams and pumping the riverbeds. Thus the underground drought phenomenon arose and the strong decrease on the basin's flow base or its ecosystem, especially the aquifers of the São Francisco system, which have the function to keep the base flow of rivers and aquatic life in the dry season. This is the main reason the water crisis and its consequences reached to this point, perennial rivers are becoming temporary and the São Francisco threats to cut its own flow. And the critical period Sobradinho supply is located in the month of January every year, according to the work of Sousa Freitas Gondim & Son (ibid). Coincidentally, this is the beginning of the rainy season in the northern semi-arid, the transposition project aims to help. There will probably be of conflict of use, including human, urban and rural consumption, among São Francisco communities and the semi-arid northern area.

Given the seriousness of the hydrological event, once again, a promising government proposal emerges, where there is a will there is a way, given the immediate interests, designs an integral planning system. Thus, the current government Temer hastens to say is that it will invest 30 billion for the New Chico project[147].

Can we give credit to "New Chico"? This is not the first government project proposing to revitalize the São Francisco. Ciro Gomes, former Minister of National Integration in the first Lula government, thinking of revitalization as a compensatory measure, announced a project and tried to implement it, but it was a complete failure. The water situation in the basin worsened in quantity and quality with great wasteful expenditure of funds by sprayed demands presented by mayors, deputies and governors, without planning and basin vision. In fact, it was funding campaigns and strengthening the allied base. A waste, for example, are the hundreds of unfinished sewage treatment plants (STPs), others not working due to technical failures, lack of resources for maintenance, many in lawsuits between municipalities by Development Company of the Valleys of the São Francisco and Parnaíba (Codevasf) and delinquent companies.

---

147 Nogueira, Edwirges (2016), 'Revitalização do São Francisco pode custar 30 bilhões', EBC Agência Brasil, accessed September, 11th 2016 at http://m. agenciabrasil.ebc.com.br/geral/noticia/2016-08/revitalizacao-do-sao-francisco-pode-custar-r-30-bilhoes.

But what do these governments and their projects understand by revitalization? It is there the main focus of a serious criticism, addressing the methodological issue inherent to the content. In the first paragraph of this text, after digressing on the natural or ecological economics, existing before the human presence on Earth, able to fully meet the demands of living beings, we question: Culture brought to Earth Politics and Economics was to make matters worse that nature was able to do so well?

Contempt for the ecosystem vision of life on Earth, by government and businessmen who control the instruments of river basin management, which leaves perspective to living beings? And focusing on the basin of the São Francisco river, what is to be expected? In general, they realize revitalization as working like dams, dredging, wastewater treatment construction targeting the urban comfort, stocking rivers with marketed fingerlings, without asking why the fish are disappearing, some of erosion containment projects with the dam among others. Many of these practices can be positive if integrated into an integration project, others already know, are ineffective or contraindicated, as the introduction of fingerlings without "history" in the river or genetic disease carriers; to spray proliferation of pesticides by aircrafts; the planting of trees without permanent care of maintenance, disassociated from fauna that is part of the ecosystem and especially when much greater deforestation is simultaneously being allowed to extensive monocultures is a scourge in itself.

That is, whenever you speak of revitalization, the basin agencies and government bodies derive a speech promising a set of disjointed works without basin logic and protection of ecosystems, gathering contractors consultants. And they carry within the ink of those words the concept of "bidding", as a testament of technical ideal by the quality of the proposal. And when they go to the field, the proposal is carried out by third party companies with expensive projects without involvement of the population, sipping billions. For the new master plan for the São Francisco Basin, the Executive Support Watershed Management Live Fish Association (AGB Peixe Vivo) agency hired a company from Portugal, in an ironic colonial relapse. Bids are executed according edicts the business ideology built, in this case, the Federation of the State of Minas Gerais Industries (FIEMG), which denies the ecosystem view of life on earth and real social participation in community empowerment.

FIEMG occupied until September 2016 the position of vice president of the Hydrographic RSF Basin Committee (CBHSF) and has full control of GB Peixe Vivo, whose board of directors is headed by former director of environmental Samarco/Vale, Anglo and MMX and also consultant FIEMG. These are on the AGB Peixe Vivo site. They are managers, companies and entities that historically detonated the environment and usually get licensing without following sustainable rules that will destroy our various river basins, such as Samarco and Vale do Rio Doce. With its total absence of ecosystem view, the current structure of the CBHSF powerful AGB Peixe Vivo, supported in agreement with the federal government and state governments, as it seems primarily aimed to ensure the economic sector that does not pay for the water they use. This is not revitalization, it is more destruction of the river. We will then refer to this central question.

The ultimate goal of this business interest in the basin committees is the control of the São Francisco water management, for economic purposes as an input of production without payment of its value. It never was, nor will it be the defense of the environment, they themselves say they are not poets. This is the "cat's leap" one more "added value" of the operating system, now common natural resources, privatize huge profits at the expense of the life of this hydrographic ecosystem and the society that dwells in it, especially the riverside.

In a market economy, it should not be socially correct that mining, agricultural business and industry pay ridiculous amounts, benefiting of the multi-purpose water and other natural resources of the basin and transfering all environmental damage and multi-purpose water as a burden to the fund company. This is to privatize and maximize profits while socializing the losses. It is also an inhibiting factor for the use of more efficient techniques in irrigation, industry, services, trade etc.

The data we have is official and available on the ANA website. The CBHSF stands out among all Brazilian committees as the one that less defends the social and environmental interests of the respective basin and society. See the official data supporting this complaint.

The table below[148] compares the average rural users rates for the three basins. No proper payments, but the basin of São Francisco is the worst in this regard:

---

148 All tables and figures presented were research collaboration of Francisco de Assis Pereira.

Table 1 k_1 adopted values in the basins of São Francisco, Paraíba do Sul and PCJ.

Basin	Standards	K.		other users
		rural users		other users
São Francisco.	Del. CBHSF No 40/2008	00.025		1
Paraiba do Sul	Del. CEIVAP No 65/2006	$0.05\ (_{Agropec}k)$		-
PCJ	Del. PCJ Committee n° 78/20017	System of Irrigation	drip	0.05
			microasperation	0.10
			central pivot	0.15
			perforated tubes	0.15
			sprinkler	0.25
			furrows	0.40
			flooding	0.50
			Not reported	0.50
		Other rural users		0.10

The following table shows the investment needs in the basin and the amounts collected with the use of water in the years 2011-2013. With such results, the São Francisco river becomes unfeasible.

Table 2 The comparison shows that charging for the use of water resources, disregarding the various resource leverage possibilities, has the average annual potential coverage BHSF's investment needs ranging from 4.0% to 8.6%.

		Values (R $ /per year)			
		2011	2012	2013	Average
Need for investment		561. 857. 602	527. 091. 208	455. 227. 902	514. 725. 571
Estimate of Revenues.	Federal Government	20 601. 325	20. 601. 325	20. 601. 325	20. 601. 325
		3.67%	3.91%	4.53%	**4.00%**
	Union and State	44. 162. 073	44. 162. 073	44. 162. 073	44. 162. 073
		7.86%	8.38%	9.70%	**8.58%**

There are absurd things, the CBHSF and its AGB Peixe Vivo Agency, under the control of FIEMG, based on an "internal judgment" is associated not to charge for water from major economic sectors. How they need to keep the system championed by AGB Peixe

Vivo, for the formal operation of CBHSF, receive compensation paid for the Transposition project. To look at the size of the contribution is a true silent mouth to the Committee, who ends up paying for water use of the basin are home users, as shown in tables and link: http://arquivos.ana.gov.br/institucional/sag/CobrancaUso/BaciaSF/Textos/Nota_Tecnica_06_11_Fev_10_Cobranca_SF.pdf

Higher values Paid VENTURE (For CNARH)	AMOUNT R$ in 2015
1. Transposition of the São Francisco River (Ministry of Integration)	12. 405. 850,00
2. Sergipe Sanitation Company	1.307.188,
3. Pernambuco Sanitation Company (COMPESA)	658.713,00
4. Bahia Minery Ltd	426.559,00
5. Pernambuco Sanitation Company	391.169,00
6. Autonomous Water and Sewer Service - SAAE / Juazeiro - BA	384.436,00
7. ALAGOAS SANITATION COMPANY	371.815,00
8. Pernambuco Sanitation Company	352.816,00
9. CARAÍBA MINERY S / A	292.206,00
10. Company Bahia Water and Sanitation S / A - EMBASA-Irecê (Pipeline Bean)	276.108,00

Venture Capital	% OF 100 LARGEST THAT PAID BY 2015	% OF TURN-OVER BY YEAR	AWARDED (2013)
BASIC SANITATION	62,0%	32%	10,0%
AGRICULTURAL BUSINESS	16,7%	16%	83,5% (*)
CODEVASFH (Various irrigation projects, except Jaíba)	13,8%	4,5%	(*) Included
MINING AND INDUSTRY	5.5%	4%	1.5%
TRANSPOSITION	0,8%	52%	5.5%
OTHERS	0.7%	1.5%	0.0%

We did, here in Minas Gerais, by the *Carta de Morrinhos* group, created in 2015, an assessment of this proposal the federal government called Project New Chico. We have the invaluable contribution of Paraiba hydrogeologist, national reference in general hydrology and semi-arid, Professor José do Patrocínio Tomaz Albuquerque. In the following lines, is part of this project evaluation New Chico that we have built together:

We disagree to the title New Chico. We prefer to be called Old Chico. So what would be sought was not a new situation for the hydrologic basin of São Francisco, but the old and natural flow condition of the river and its tributaries.

The revival call is placed in very vague terms. It just says that it involves the recovery of degraded areas, restoration of riparian forests and sanitation deployment in all 507 cities that make up the basin of São Francisco. They do not specify where they are and what is considered as degraded areas. Certainly, the numerous irrigation perimeters established in deforested areas are not included in them, these indeed are the major consumers of water resources components of the fluvial drainage basin, especially the segments provided by its groundwater, its base flow. Consumption is higher than the recharge capacity, circulation and discharge of the basin aquifers, especially the components of the São Francisco Aquifer System. This is the biggest reason for the reduction in the average flow of the São Francisco and regulating capacity of its surface reservoirs. Indirectly, the document says that "one of the reasons for this degradation is anthropization, also the disorderly occupation of land." But it does not say where and how they will intervene to put the occupation in environmental and socioeconomic axes. We know that the concept of revitalization should be related to the supply of water from the basin, inseparable from the preservation of its ecosystems. Employing the term replenish the amount of water. This is because, as much as they could implement actions to restore environmental conditions, historical and natural basin, it could not enhance anything, but rather just recover. Human action cannot change the conditions for the better, the water yield of a watershed, i.e. the components infiltration and direct runoff (the R&R of the water balance equation) resulting from the average precipitation (P) which focuses on the actual evapotranspiration (ETR), historically recorded in the basin. This balance can be handled, and the reduced infiltration result in an increase of the direct runoff (runoff), although with increasing intensity of the surface flow. But always keeping the same balance. This is what happens: the direct flows of rivers are increasingly more and faster, because they are made in a shorter period of time, since the base flow is impaired. All this in its own natural terms, without human intervention. But if the society, in order to meet their water needs, intervenes in the (I+R), building dams or drilling wells to capture it, there will be reduction in average natural supply, caused by evaporation losses. This is what happens, for example, Sobradinho, whose average inflow is (or was) of 2,706 m³/s regularized discharge does not exceed 1715 m³/s. The excessive pumping groundwater resulting in decrease of the base flow, reducing flow before recorded in fluviometric stations, the pumped flow exceeds the natural recharge, the flow and, therefore, their discharge into rivers and in the case of coastal water, also the sea. This is the cause of reduced natural inflow to reservoirs' surface and, consequently, its settlement flows, increasingly dependent on direct runoff, immediately subordinating to the rainfall. Contrary to recently said IBAMA/SE, there is an increasingly dependence on the river flows amount of foregone rain in the basin, since the beginning of its time, was perennial due to the significant contribution of the base flow, becomes intermittent or ephemeral. And if it does not rain, the river does not flow as usual. Therefore, the flow of recovery actions should relate to the restoration of the base flow, which is being reduced by the pumping wells or funding "a trickle", used in the main consumer of the basin, irrigation (about 80% of the total available), and renewable reserves of groundwater are fully used and, more than that, it is also used part of the mentioned permanent reserve. Therefore, measures that, perchance, may be taken in the quantitative revitalization proposal of the São Francisco river should include the additional groundwater base flow.

Finally, an odd statement by Mr. Anivaldo Miranda, president of CBHSF that "among the activities that require more water from the São Francisco River, is Transposition". Until recently, the transposition was seen as a project that impacted the flow of the river after Sobradinho, representing something less than 1.5% of the regulated flow, as if, in the stretch between Sobradinho and Xingó, there was no conflict of usage between power generation (which in principle uses the entire flow regularized by Sobradinho) and consumptive uses, including, irrigation, human, urban and rural supply. (José do Patrocínio Tomaz Albuquerque).

***

With this statement, we bring our story to an end, we connect our research to the valuable work done by the Manuelzão project, we give voice to the river people and call for the preservation of the beautiful and miraculous river we have learned to love. Save Opará!

REFERENCES

Andrade, Manoel. C (1984), *Poder político e produção do espaço*. Recife: Massangana.

Aleixo, Caroline, Portilho, Carolina (2014), 'Diretor de parque diz que principal nascente do Rio São Francisco secou', accessed September, 20 2015 at http://g1.globo.com/mg/centro-oeste/noticia/2014/09/diretor-de-parque-diz-que-principal-nascente-do-rio-sao-francisco-secou.html.

Antropozoide (2007), 'Retomada do povo indígena Truká: em busca da homologação contínua', 23 july, accessed May, 20 2015 at http://antropozoide.blogspot.com.br/2007/07/recente-retomada-truka-oficializada-no.html.

Arcanjo, J.A. (2003), *Toré e identidade étnica: os Pipipã dekambixuru* (índios da Serra Negra. 2003. 162 f. Dissertação (Mestrado em Antropologia) – Centro de Filosofia e Ciências Humanas, Universidade Federal de Pernambuco, Recife.

Áries, Paul (2005), *Décroissance ou barbárie*, Paris: Editions Golias.

ASA Brasil (2009), 'ASA na mídia', accessed January, 4, 2015 at http://www.asabrasil.org.br/imprensa/asa-na-midia?artigo_id=9391.

Azevedo, Luiz Gabriel Todt de, Porto, Rubem La Laina, Méllo Júnior, Ariosvaldo Vieira; Pereira, Juliana Garrido, Arrobas, Daniele La Porta; Noronha, Luiz Correa e Pereira (2005), *Transferência de Água entre Bacias Hidrográficas*, Brasília: Banco Mundial.

Bahia Notícias (2007), 'Rio São Francisco: maratona pelo nordeste' accessed April, 12, 2016 at http://www.bahianoticias.com.br/noticia/2159-rio-sao-francisco-maratona-pelo nordeste.html.

Bandeira, Luiz Alberto Moniz (2000) *O feudo: a Casa da Torre de Garcia d'Ávila: da conquista dos sertões à independência do Brasil*. Rio de Janeiro: Civilização Brasileira.

BARBOSA, Wallace de Deus (2001), *Um Embate de Culturas: análise de processos políticos e estratégias sócio-culturais na construção das identidades Kambiwá e Pipipã*. 2001, 293 f.Tese (Doutorado) – PPGAS/MN – UFRJ, Rio de Janeiro.

Barreto Filho, Henyo Trindade (1999), *Invenção ou Renascimento? Gênese de uma Sociedade Indígena Contemporânea no Nordeste.* Oliveira, João Pacheco de. *A Viagem da Volta: etnicidade, política e reelaboração cultural no Nordeste Indígena.* Rio de Janeiro: Contra Capa Livraria.

Batista. Mércia Rejane Rangel (2005), *Descobrindo e recebendo heranças: as lideranças Truká.* 2005. 265 f. Tese (Doutorado em Antropologia) – Programa de Pós-Graduação em Antropologia Social, Museu Nacional, da Universidade Federal do Rio de Janeiro – UFRJ, Rio de Janeiro.

Besson-Girad, Jean-Claude (2005), *Decrescendo Cantabile: Petit Manuel pour une décroissance harmonique*, Lyon: Paragon.

Bocato-Franco, Alan, (2013), Para Compreender o Decrescimento, Carta Capital, accessed 05 november 2016 at http://www.cartacapital.com.br/blogs/outras-palavras/para-compreender-o-201cdecrescimento201d-3687.html.

Boccato-franco, A. A. (2012), 'O decrescimento no Brasil'. In: Léna, P.; Nascimento, E. P. do (Eds.). *Enfrentando os limites do crescimento*: sustentabilidade, decrescimento e prosperidade, Rio de Janeiro, Garamond, 2012. p. 269–288.

Calmon, Pedro. *História da Casa da Torre* (s/d), Rio de Janeiro: José Olympio Ed.

Campos, José Nilson B (2014) Secas e políticas públicas no semiárido: ideias, pensadores e períodos. *Estudos Avançados*. vol.28 no.82 São Paulo Oct./Dec. 2014.

Carta Maior (2006), 'Entidades repudiam declaração de Lula sobre povos tradicionais', accessed February, 20 2016 at http://www.cartamaior.com.br/?/Editoria/Meio-Ambiente/Entidades-repudiam-declaracao-de-Lula-sobre-povos-tradicionais/3/12236.

Carta Maior (2015), 'Exército agiliza obra no país e as empreiteiras se queixam', accessed May, 22 2015 at http://cartamaior.com.br/?/Editoria/Economia/Exercito-agiliza-obras-no-pais-e-as-empreiteiras-se-queixam/7/33329.

Cunha, Euclides da (1984), *Os Sertões*, São Paulo: Três, Biblioteca.

Cunha, Euclides da (2001), *Os Sertões*. São Paulo: Ateliê Editorial.

Cunha, Euclides da (2010), *Os Sertões*, Rio de Janeiro: Centro Edelstein de Pesquisas Sociais.

Cunha, Manuel Correia de Andrade (1984), *O sentido da colonização*. São Paulo: Comunicações e Ed.

Daly, Herman E. (1977) *Steady- Economics*, Washington, DC: Island Press.

Daly, Herman E. (1996), *Beyond Growth: The Economics of Sustainable Development*, Boston: Beacon Press.

Dias, Débora, Castro, Gigi, Said, Magnólia, Gonçalves, Adelaide (Eds) (2008), *A vida por um rio*. *Frente Cearense Por Uma Nova Culturada Água e Contra a Transposição das Águas do Rio São Francisco*, Fortaleza.

Direito do Estado (2011), 'Investigações apuram envolvimento de militares em fraudes nas obras do PAC', accessed September, 10, 2016 at http://www.direitodoestado.com.br/noticias/investigacoes-apuram-envolvimento-de-militares-em-fraudes-nas-obras-do-pac.

Eco Debate (2015), 'Rio São Francisco: Os impactos da transposição nas comunidades do Semiárido. Entrevista com Roberto Malvezzi, o Gogó', accessed May, 14 2015 at http://www.ecodebate.com.br/2010/04/09/rio-sao-francisco-os-impactos-da-transposicao-nas-comunidades-do-semi-arido-entrevista-com-roberto-malvezzi-o-gogo.

Environmental Ethics (2016) The Debate over Anthropocentrism, accessed 9 october 2016 at http://science.jrank.org/pages/9156/Environmental-Ethics-Debate-over-Anthropocentrism. html.

Fisher, William F. (1999), 'Introduction', *Cultural Survival Quarterly*, Vol 23, Issue 3, Fall.

_____. 'Going under: indigenous peoples and the struggle against large dams', Cultural Survival Quartely, Vol 23, Issue 3, Fall 1999.

Folha Uol (2007), 'Artigo de Geddel motiva da CNBB a bispo', acessed May, 11 2015 at http://www1.folha.uol.com.br/fsp/brasil/fc1512200725.htm.

Folha Uol (2013), 'Dilma cede a pressão dos ruralistas e rifa os direitos indígenas, diz antropólogo da USP', accessed January, 14 2016 at http://www1.folha.uol.com.br/poder/2013/07/1310677-dilma-cede-a-pressao-dos-ruralistas-e-rifa-os-direitos-indigenas-diz-antropologa-da-usp.shtml>.

Folha Uol (2013), 'Inacabada, transposição deve ter dois novos eixos' accessed October, 14 2015 at http://www1.folha.uol.com.br/fsp/poder/168630-inacabada-transposicao-deve-ter-dois-novos-eixos.shtml.

Freitas, M. A. S, Gondim Filho, Joaquim Guedes Corrêa (2004), 'Disponibilidade Hídrica do Sistema Formado pelos Reservatórios Três Marias e Sobradinho na Bacia do São Francisco Para Fins de Alocação de Água', *Anais do VII Simpósio de Recursos Hídricos do Nordeste*, Nov./Dez./2004, São Luís/MA.

Freitas, Guilherme (2016), 'Eduardo Viveiros de Castro: o que se vê no Brasil hoje é uma ofensa feroz contra os índios', Jornal O Globo, accessed September,3 2016 at http://oglobo.globo.com/cultura/livros/eduardo-viveiros-de-castro-que-se-ve-no-brasil-hoje-uma-ofensiva-feroz-contra-os-indios-17261624.

G1 Globo.com (2015) '7 das 10 maiores empreiteiras tiveram executivos investigados na lava-jato', accessed September, 10, 2016 at http://g1.globo.com/politica/operacao-lava-jato/noticia/2015/06/7-das-10-maiores-empreiteiras-tiveram-executivos-investigados-na-lava-jato.html.

Galvão, Sebastião de Vasconcellos (1987) *Diccionario chorografico, historico e estatistico de Pernambuco*, Recife.

Georgescu- Roegen, Nicholas (1975), La décroissance: Entropie – Écologie – Économie, Paris: Éditions Sang de la terre.

Heinberg, Richard (1997) "Was Civilization a Mistake?" in *Green Anarchist*, Autumn.

Henkes, Silviana L (2014) *A política, o direito e o desenvolvimento*: um estudo sobre a transposição do rio São Francisco. Rev. Direito GV, São Paulo, v. 10, n. 2, p. 497-534.

Índios Online (2007) 'Luta popular desmascara a transposição', accessed April,11, 2016 at http://www.indiosonline.net/luta_popular_desmascara_a_transposicao/.

JC Online (2014), 'Durante visita de dilma, indígenas da tribo Truká bloqueiam BR 428 em protesto', accessed October, 20, 2015 at http://jconline.ne10.uol.com.br/canal/politica/pernambuco/noticia/2014/05/13/durante-visita-de-dilma-indigenas-da-tribo-truka-bloqueiam-br-428-em-protesto-127856.php.

Jornal Folha de São Paulo (2015), Corrupção generalizada, accessed August,10, 2016 at http://opiniao.estadao.com.br/noticias/geral,corrupcao-generalizada,1814142.

Jornal Hoje (2015), Final da obra de transposição do rio São Francisco está prevista para 2007, accessed September,3, 2016 at http://g1.globo.com/jornal-hoje/noticia/2015/07/final-da-obra-de-transposicao-do-rio-sao-francisco-esta-prevista-para-2017.html.

Kauffman, Jean- Claude (2005), Casseroles, amour at crises. Ce que cuisinier veut dire, Paris: Armand Colin.

Kuri, Lorelai (2004), 'Homens de ciência no Brasil: impérios coloniais e circulação de informações (1780-1810)', *História, Ciências, Saúde* - Manguinhos, accessed September,22, 2016.

Lamounier, Bolivar (2016), Cinco razões para darmos adeus à Dilma, Jornal Folha de São Paulo, accessed August,22, 2016 at http://www1.folha.uol.com.br/opiniao/2016/08/1807611-cinco-razoes-para-darmos-adeus-a-dilma.shtml.

Latouche, S. (2009) *Pequeno Tratado do Decrescimento Sereno*, São Paulo, WMF Martins Fontes.

Lima, Geddel Vieira (2007), 'O inimigo número 1 da Democracia', Jornal Folha de São Paulo, accessed May, 1, 2015 at http://www1.folha.uol.com.br/fsp/opiniao/fz1012200708.htm.

Maldoz, Paulo (2008), 'Presidente Lula e Dom Cappio, na Roda Viva da História', DIAS, Débora; CASTRO, Gigi; SAID, Magnólia; GONÇALVES, Adelaide (Eds.). *A vida por um rio.* Frente Cearense Por Uma Nova Culturada Água e Contra a Transposição das Águas do Rio São Francisco, Fortaleza.

Marengo, José A; Nobre, Carlos A; Salati, Eneas; Ambrizzi, T. (2007), *Mudanças Climáticas Globais e Efeitos sobre a Biodiversidade.* Brasil:Ministério do Meio Ambiente.

Marengo, José A. (2008) 'Água e mudanças climáticas'. *Estud. av.* [online], 22 (63), pp.83-96 accessed May, 24, 2016.

Ministério da Infra Estrutura (2016), 'Rio São Francisco recebeu 1,9 milhão de peixes nativos em 2015' (2016), accessed February,14, 2016 at http://www.brasil.gov.br/infraestrutura/2016/02/ rio-sao-francisco-recebeu-1-9-milhao-de-peixes-nativos-em-2015.

Monteiro, Eliana de Barros (2008), *Eu* já vi água ir embora ... com natureza não se mexe ... eu já vi água ir embora: os Truká (PE) "grandes projetos", o sentido da territorialidade no exercício da cidadania indígena contemporânea. 2008, 207 f. Dissertação (Mestrado em Antropologia) – CCLH, Universidade Federal de Pernambuco, Recife.

Moura, A. (1993), *O sumidouro do São Francisco: subterrâneos da Cultura Brasileira*. Rio de Janeiro: Ed. Tempo Brasileiro.

Nabarro, David (2016), 'Conselheiro especial de Ban Ki-moon para a Agenda de Desenvolvimento Sustentável 2030', *Folha de São Paulo*, setembro de 2016.

Nascimento, José Leonardo, Facioli, Valentin (2003), *Juízos Críticos. Os Sertões e os olhares de sua época*, São Paulo: Ed. Unesp.

Neto, Nivaldo Aureliano Leo (2015), '"Nós somos os donos": conflitos socioambientais entre os índios Pipipá de Kambixuru e o ICMBIO no sertão de Pernambuco', accessed May, 20, 2016 at http://eventos.livera.com.br/traba lho/98-1020291_25_06_2015_10-44-30_9459.PDF.

Neves, C. Cardoso, A.P. A Experiência Internacional com Projetos de Transposição de Águas: lições para o do rio São Francisco. XXIX Encontro Nacional de Engenharia de

Produção. A Engenharia de Produção e o Desenvolvimento Sustentável: Integrando Tecnologia e Gestão. Salvador, BA, Brasil, 06 a 09 de outubro de 2009: <http://www.abepro.org.br/ biblioteca/enegep2009_TN_STO_099_665_12814.pdf>.

Nogueira, Edwirges (2016), 'Revitalização do São Francisco pode custar 30 bilhões', EBC Agência Brasil, accessed September, 11, 2016 at http://m.agenciabrasil.ebc.com.br/geral/noticia/2016-08/ revitalizacao-do-sao-francisco-pode-custar-r-30-bilhoes.

Oliveira, Kelly Emanuele de (2013) *Diga ao povo que avance! Movimento indígena no nordeste.* Recife: Fundação Joaquim Nabuco, Editora Massangana.

OPIT (2007), *No reino da Assunção, reina Truká. Organização das professoras Truká.* Belo Horizonte: FALE/UFMG, SECAD/MEC.

Panfleto Pau de Colher (2014), Articulação Popular São Francisco Vivo, accessed 10 september 2014 at http://saofranciscovivo.org.br/site/wp-content/uploads/2014/12/panfleto-pau-de-colher.pdf.

Pierson, Donald (1972), *O homem do Vale do São Francisco.* Rio de Janeiro: Superintendência do Vale do São Francisco, Ministério do Interior, Fundação IBGE, 1972.

Pompa, Cristina, (2002), *Religião como tradução: missionários, Tupi e Tapuia no Brasil colonia*l. Bauru, SP: EDUSC/ ANPOCS.

Projeto Manuelzão (2007), 'A caravana em defesa do São Francisco e do SEMI', accessed January, 12, 2015 at http://www.manuelzao.ufmg.br/assets/files/Biblioteca_Virtual/A-Caravana-em defesa-do-Sao-Francisco-e-do-Semi.pdf.

Raine, Alan, Foster, John, Potts, Jason (1971), 'The Entropy Law and the Economic Process', *Ecological Complexity*, accessed September, 14, 2016 at http://www.sciencedirect.com/science/article/pii/S1476945X07000104.

Relatório Brundtland, Nosso Futuro Comum (1987), accessed August, 30 2016 at https://ambiente.wordpress.com/2011/03/22/relatrio-brundtland-a-verso-original/.

Relatório-denúncia 'Aceleração do crescimento na bacia do rio São Francisco: o traçado de conflitos e injustiças sociais e ambientais' (2008), accessed May, 20 2015 at http://docplayer.com.br/7108933-Aceleracao-do-crescimento-na-bacia-do-rio-sao-francisco-o-tracado-de-conflitos-e-injusticas-sociais-e-ambientais.html.

Relatório de denúncia CIMI (2007), 'Povos indígenas impactados com a transposição do rio São Francisco, accessed September, 15, 2015 at http://www.cimi.org.br/pub/publicacoes/1241549933_relatapoinmetransp.pdf.

141

Sen, Amartya (1999), *Sobre ética e economia*, São Paulo: cia das letras.

Scott, Parry (2009), *Negociações e resistências persistentes: agricultores e a barragem de Itaparica num contexto de descaso planejado*. Recife: Ed. Universitária da UFPE.

Spinelli, Miguel (2006) Questões Fundamentais da Filosofia Grega. São Paulo: Loyola.

Terra Brasil (2005), 'Após dias termina a greve de fome de Dom Cappio', accessed December, 20, 2015 at http://noticias.terra. com.br/brasil/noticias/0,OI697770-EI306,00-Apos+dias+-termina+gr%20 eve+de+fome+de+Dom+Cappio.html.

Transposição: águas da ilusão (2007), Revista Transposição Final, accessed May,4, 2016 at https://psicologiadareligiao.files.wordpress.com/2007/12/revista_transposicao_web1.pdf.

Trata Brasil (2015), Situação saneamento no Brasil, acessed Septembe, 5, 2016 at http://www.tratabrasil.org.br/saneamento-no-brasil.

Tribunal de Contas da União (2011), 'Relatório de Auditoria', accessed September, 7, 2015 at http://tcu.jusbrasil.com.br/jurisprudencia/316486543/2953920102/inteiro-teor-316486626.

Tribunal de Contas da União (2012), 'Diário Oficial', processo 037.773/2011, accessed April, 20, 2015 at http://www.jusbrasil.com.br/diarios/DOU/2012/01/25.

Tribunal de Contas da União (2015), 'TCU fiscaliza ações de recuperação do Programa de Revitalização da Bacia Hidrográfica do Rio São Francisco', accessed May, 28, 2016 at http://portal.tcu.gov.br/imprensa/noticias/tcu-fiscaliza-acoes-de-recuperacao-do-programa-de-revitalizacao-da-bacia-hidrografica-do-rio-sao-francisco.htm.

Revista Exame (2016), Um guia para o Brasil pós-PT, accessed September, 04, 2016 at http://exame.abril.com.br/revista-exame/edicoes/1114/.

Viana, V.M. (1999), Envolvimento sustentável e conservação das florestas brasileiras, accessed October, 02, 2016 at http://www.scielo.br/pdf/asoc/n5/n5a21.pdf.

Waldman, Maurício (2005), *Meio Ambiente e Antropologia*. São Paulo: Senac.

www.ingramcontent.com/pod-product-compliance
Lightning Source LLC
Chambersburg PA
CBHW032354280326
41935CB00008B/563